DOING HISTORY:
A Strategic Guide to
Document-Based Questions

Global Studies
Edition

by Malcolm Jensen

aim higher!®

Great Source Education Group
A division of Houghton Mifflin Company
Wilmington, MA

www.greatsource.com

Staff Credits:

Editorial
Robert D. Shepherd
Laura Sanderson
Trina Coleron

Design
Amanda Sylvester

Production
AARTPACK, Inc.

Research & Writing
Cecelia Munzenmaier
Daniel Rosen
Richard Brent Goff

Acknowledgments

The publisher gratefully acknowledges permission granted for use of materials reprinted in this book. The authors and editors have made every effort to trace the ownership of all copyrighted pieces found in this book and to make full acknowledgment for their use. (Acknowledgments are continued on page 121.)

First Edition

Printed in the United States of America

3 4 5 6 7 8 9 10   DBH   10 09 08 07

International Standard Book Number-13: 978-1-58171-529-3
International Standard Book Number-10: 1-58171-529-3

CONTENTS

PRETESTS

This unit contains two Pretests.

You will have an hour and a half to complete each test.

PRETEST A: DOCUMENT-BASED QUESTION

Historical Background:

Governments serve many purposes. The Constitution of the United States, for example, begins with a sentence that suggests the following purposes for the formation of the United States government: "to form a more perfect union, establish justice, insure domestic tranquility, provide for the common defense, promote the general welfare, and secure the blessings of liberty to ourselves and our posterity." Over the centuries, many forms of government have evolved, of which representative government as found in the United States is but one. Many of the forms of government practiced around the world today—including **monarchy,** or rule by a king, queen, or emperor; **oligarchy,** or rule by a group of elders; **democracy,** or rule by the people; **totalitarianism,** or absolute rule by a single leader or faction; and **republican government,** or rule by elected officials, had their origins in the ancient world. Throughout the centuries, people have debated which system of government is the best.

Task:

Write an essay about government and law in ancient societies. What reasons did the philosophers of ancient times give for preferring one form of government to another? How were these reasons related to a particular view of human nature? Give examples from the documents to support your argument.

Before you write your essay, study the documents that follow and answer the scaffolding questions about them.

Part A: Scaffolding Questions

Directions:

Using information from the documents and your knowledge of social studies, answer the question that follows each document. Your answers will help you write the essay in Part B.

Pericles lived from 495 BCE–429 BCE. He was the leader of Athens during its golden age of democracy. During this time, Athens fought the Peloponnesian War against Sparta and its allies. At the end of the first year of fighting, Pericles gave a speech to commemorate the Athenians who had fallen in the war.

> *[W]e are called a democracy, for the [power] is in the hands of the many and not of the few. But while there exists equal justice to all . . . , the claim of excellence is also recognized; and when a citizen is in any way distinguished, he is preferred [for] public service, not as a matter of privilege, but as the reward of merit. Neither is poverty an obstacle, but a man may benefit his country [however poor or little known he may be]. . . .[W]e are prevented from doing wrong by respect for the authorities and for the laws, having a particular regard [for those laws which exist to protect the powerless,] as well as those unwritten laws which bring upon [those who break them the disrepute of their fellow citizens.]*

Excerpt from Pericles' Funeral Oration

1. According to Pericles, what advantages are there in a democratic form of government?

_____

_____

_____

Plato (c. 427 BCE–347 BCE) was a Greek philosopher who was a student of Socrates. In his book, *The Republic*, he expressed the following opinion about democratic government:

> *Why, that all those . . . Sophists . . . teach nothing but the opinion of the many, that is to say, the opinions of their assemblies; and this is their wisdom. I might compare them to a man who should study the tempers and desires of a mighty strong beast who is fed by him—he would learn how to approach and handle him, also at what times and from what causes he is*

> *dangerous or the reverse, and what is the meaning of his several cries, and by what sounds, when another utters them, he is soothed or infuriated; and you may suppose further, that when, by continually attending upon him, he has become perfect in all this, he calls his knowledge wisdom, and makes of it a system or art, which he proceeds to teach, although he has no real notion of what he means by the principles or passions of which he is speaking, but calls this honorable and that dishonorable, or good or evil, or just or unjust, all in accordance with the tastes and tempers of the great brute. Good he pronounces to be that in which the beast delights and evil to be that which he dislikes; and he can give no other account.*

Excerpt from Plato's *Republic*

2. To what does Plato compare "the many" (that is, the mass of people)? What does Plato think of basing one's principles on the will of the many?

_____

_____

Aristotle was a student of Plato. In the following excerpt, he is writing about the advantages and disadvantages of the oligarchical government of Sparta.

> *Again, the council of elders is not free from defects. It may be said that the elders are good men and well trained in manly virtue; and that, therefore, there is an advantage to the state in having them. But that judges of important causes should hold office for life is a disputable thing, for the mind grows old as well as the body. And when men have been educated in such a manner that even the legislator himself cannot trust them, there is real danger. Many of the elders are well known to have taken bribes and to have been guilty of partiality in public affairs. And therefore they ought not to be irresponsible; yet at Sparta they are so.*

Excerpt from *The Politics of Aristotle*

3. What does Aristotle see as the advantages and disadvantages of government officers being appointed for life?

_____

_____

Cicero (106 BCE–43 BCE) was a Roman politician, a writer and speaker whose speeches have been used by orators as a model for more than two thousand years. In the following excerpts, Cicero analyzes the advantages of different forms of government.

[Of all the different forms of government,] I must confess I prefer the royal one, and praise that as the first and best. In this, which I here choose to call the primitive form of government, I find the title of father attached to that of king, to express that he watches over the citizens as over his children, and endeavors rather to preserve them in freedom than reduce them to slavery. So that it is more advantageous for those who are [poor] to be supported by the care of one excellent and eminently powerful man. The nobles here present themselves, who profess that they can do all this in much better style; for they say that there is much more wisdom in many than in one, and at least as much faith and equity. And, last of all, come the people, who cry with a loud voice, that they will render obedience neither to the one nor to the few; that…nothing is so dear as liberty; and that all men who serve either kings or nobles are deprived of it. Thus, the kings attract us by affection, the nobles by talent, the people by liberty; and in the comparison it is hard to choose the best.

Excerpt from *On the Republic*

4. What advantages does Cicero identify for each form of government? Which one does he prefer and why?

_____

_____

_____

_____

Claudius was Emperor of Rome from 41 CE–54 CE. In this speech, reported by the historian Tacitus, Claudius urges the Senate to accept members from the province of Gaul.

What was the ruin of Sparta and Athens, but this, that mighty as they were in war, they spurned from them as aliens those whom they had conquered? Our founder Romulus, on the other hand, was so wise that he fought as enemies and then hailed as fellow-citizens several

Excerpt from Tacitus's *Annals*

5. According to Claudius, what distinguishes the Roman Empire?

_____

_____

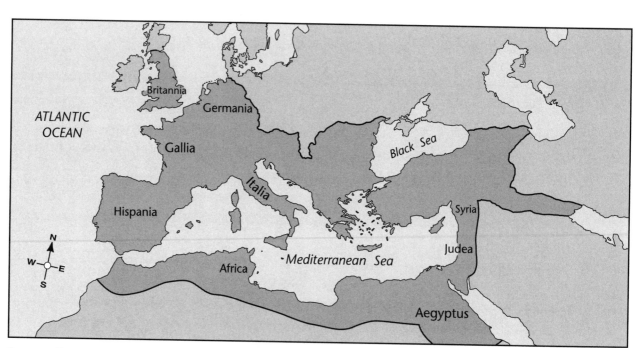

Roman Empire, c. 120 CE

6. At its height, the Roman Empire spanned three continents. Think about the statement made by the Emperor Claudius, above. What do you think the Roman government did that made it possible for them to maintain such an enormous empire?

_____

_____

K'ung-fu-tzu, popularly known in the West as Confucius (551 BCE–479 BCE), was a philosopher whose teachings dominated Chinese thought for centuries. Han Fei-tzu (died in 233 BCE) was a philosopher of a later era who grew up studying Confucius. Han Fei-tzu founded a new school of thought called the Legalists. Both Confucius and Han Fei-tzu lived under absolute rulers. Confucius believed that a good state was one founded upon the virtue of the ruler:

> *The Master said, "If the people are governed by laws and punishment is used to maintain order, they will try to avoid the punishment but have no sense of shame. If they are governed by virtue and rules of propriety [ritual] are used to maintain order, they will have a sense of shame and will become good as well."*

Confucius, *Analects*

Han Fei-tzu did not agree:

> *When a sage governs a state, he does not rely on the people to do good out of their own will. Instead, he sees to it that they are not allowed to do what is not good. If he relies on people to do good out of their own will, within the borders of the state not even ten persons can be counted on [to do good]. Yet, if one sees to it that they are not allowed to do what is not good, the whole state can be brought to uniform order. Whoever rules should consider the majority and set the few aside: He should not devote his attention to virtue, but to law.*

Excerpt from Han Fei-tzu, *Legalist Views on Good Government*

7. What is the nature of the disagreement between Confucius and Han Fei-tzu?

_____

_____

_____

Part B: Essay Response

Directions:

Use your answers from Part A to write an essay comparing and contrasting the views held in ancient societies regarding what constitutes good government. In your essay, cite the opinions expressed in the documents you have studied.

In your essay, remember to include
- an introduction, or opening paragraph, that tells your answer to the question;
- two or three body paragraphs that give examples from the documents;
- a conclusion, or ending paragraph, that tells your answer to the question and lists your examples.

STOP

PRETEST B: DOCUMENT-BASED QUESTION

Historical Background:

In 1933 Adolf Hitler came to power in Germany. One policy of Hitler's Nazi Party was anti-Semitism. The Nazis blamed Germany's defeat in World War I and its subsequent economic troubles on Jews and promised to act against them. Jews were stripped of German citizenship and then arrested and herded into concentration camps. In 1942, the Nazis formalized their plan to murder the Jews of Europe in gas chambers at concentration camps such as Auschwitz, Buchenwald, and Dachau.

Task:

Write an essay about what you know about the Holocaust and how you know it. Use your knowledge of social studies and the documents you examine to inform your answer. In your answer, give examples from the documents.

Before writing your essay, study the documents that follow and answer the scaffolding questions about them.

Part A: Scaffolding Questions

Directions:

Using information from the documents and your knowledge of social studies, answer the question that follows each document. Your answers will help you write the essay in Part B.

Margaret Bourke-White was a photojournalist. At the end of World War II, she took this photograph of survivors of the concentration camp at Buchenwald. The survivors are wearing the striped uniforms of camp prisoners.

1. What does the photograph tell you about the treatment of people in the concentration camp?

_____

_____

_____

_____

In January 1939, Adolf Hitler gave a speech to the Reichstag, the German parliament, in which he suggested his plan for the Jews.

> *If [the Jews of the world] should succeed once again in plunging the nations into a world war, then the result will not be the victory of [the Jews], but [the complete] annihilation of the Jewish race in Europe!*

Reichstag speech, January 30, 1939

2. What does Hitler want the German people to believe about the Jews?

_____

_____

_____

Report No. 51 of Reichsfuehrer-SS Himmler to Hitler about Mass Executions in the East, 1942

	August	September	October	November
Prisoners executed after interrogation	2,100	1,400	1,596	2,731
Accomplices of guerrilla and guerrilla suspects executed	1,198	3,020	6,333	3,706
Jews executed	31,246	165,282	95,735	70,948
Villages and localities burned down or destroyed	35	12	20	92

Heinrich Himmler was, next to Hitler, the most powerful man in Nazi Germany. Himmler was head of the SS, the armed wing of the Nazi Party, which included its secret police, and was also in charge of setting up concentration camps and the extermination of the Jews. In 1943, he sent a report to Hitler about the pace of executions in the East.

3. What does the information tell you about the Nazis' policy toward the Jews?

_____

_____

_____

> *We came to the question: what to [do] with the women and children? I decided to find a clear solution here as well. I did not consider myself justified to exterminate the men—that is, to kill them or have them killed—and allow the avengers of our sons and grandsons in the form of their children to grow up. The difficult decision had to be taken to make this people disappear from the earth.*

Also in 1943, Himmler, in a speech, offered his explanation of why the Nazis were killing women and children, in addition to men.

4. How does Himmler justify the execution of women and children?

_____

_____

_____

Outside a concentration camp

5. This photograph, showing a pile of shoes, was taken outside a concentration camp. Where do you think the shoes came from? What does the size of the pile indicate about what is happening inside the camp?

_____

_____

_____

Anne Frank (1929–1945) was a young Jewish girl whose family left Germany for the Netherlands. After the Nazis invaded the Netherlands, the Frank family went into hiding for more than two years. In 1944, they were discovered and arrested by the Nazis. Anne and her sister were sent first to Auschwitz, then to Bergen-Belsen, where they died in a typhus epidemic in March 1945, two months before the end of the war in Europe. After their arrest, neighbors who had assisted the Franks searched the hiding place and found Anne's diary, which she kept during her years in hiding.

Anne Frank

We're much too young to deal with these problems, but they keep thrusting themselves on us until, finally, we're forced to think up a solution, though most of the time our solutions crumble when faced with the facts. It's difficult in times like these: ideals, dreams and cherished hopes rise within us, only to be crushed by grim reality. It's a wonder I haven't abandoned all my ideals, they seem so absurd and impractical. Yet I cling to them because I still believe, in spite of everything, that people are truly good at heart.

It's utterly impossible for me to build my life on a foundation of chaos, suffering and death. I see the world being slowly transformed into a wilderness, I hear the approaching thunder that, one day, will destroy us too, I feel the suffering of millions. And yet, when I look up at the sky, I somehow feel that everything will change for the better, that this cruelty too shall end, that peace and tranquility will return once more.

From Anne Frank's diary, June 15, 1944

6. Why do you think Anne Frank thought, despite the actions of the Nazis, that "people are truly good at heart"?

_____

_____

_____

Part B: Essay Response

Directions:

Use your answers from Part A to write an essay about the Holocaust. In your essay, explain what the Nazi policy was, how it was carried out, how it affected its victims, and how we know that the Holocaust occurred.

In your essay, remember to include

- an introduction, or opening paragraph, that tells your answer to the question;
- two or three body paragraphs that give examples from the documents;
- a conclusion, or ending paragraph, that tells your answer to the question and lists your examples.

_____

_____

_____

_____

_____

_____

_____

_____

_____

_____

_____

_____

_____

_____

_____

_____

_____

_____

_____

_____

_____

_____

_____

_____

_____

_____

_____

STOP

LESSON 1.1: UNDERSTANDING DOCUMENT-BASED QUESTIONS

What Are Document-Based Questions?

Although the phrases "document-based question" and "document-based essay" may sound complicated, they can easily be understood when they are broken into parts. A **document** is anything written or printed that provides facts, or information, such as a map, letter, or a photograph. A **document-based question (DBQ)** is a question that is about one or more of these written or printed source materials. Some document-based questions ask for specific information and can be answered in one or two sentences. Others require you to take information from several documents and to use this information in an extended piece of writing called an **essay.**

Documents

Documents can be primary or secondary sources. **Primary sources** are original documents from a particular time in the past, such as photographs, letters, and newspaper articles. Other primary sources include illustrations, cartoons, posters, maps, and political documents like the Constitution. **Secondary sources** are documents that are not from the era that they cover. Examples include a graph made from historical data and an article based on facts taken from primary sources.

Types of Question on DBQ Tests

A typical DBQ test contains documents, scaffolding questions, and an essay question. A **scaffolding question** is one that asks for a specific piece of information from a document. A scaffolding question usually deals with a single document and can be answered in one or two short sentences. The questions on pages 3–7 and 11–15 of the Pretests are examples of scaffolding questions. Answering these questions will help you to build up a store of information that you can use to write an essay.

An **essay question** is one that requires a response containing more than one paragraph. To answer an essay question on a DBQ exam, you have to draw information from several documents. You begin by coming up with a **thesis statement**—a single sentence that answers the essay question in a general way. Then, you use information from the documents that backs up, or **supports**, your thesis statement. The questions on pages 8 and 16 are examples of essay questions.

General Strategies for DBQ Tests

Whenever you take a DBQ test, like the Pretests in Unit 1, begin by reading the test directions carefully. Then read the historical background information and ask yourself, "What do I already know about this subject or era?" The chances are good that you have already studied the era and know something about it. Next, read the task carefully. This part of the test directions tells what your essay will be about. Pay particular attention to key action words that say what you are supposed to do. Here are some action words that appear in test directions:

Analyze: break something into its parts, describe the parts, and show how the parts are related to one another

Compare: tell about the similarities between two things

Contrast: tell about the differences between two things

Describe: tell about something in detail

Interpret: explain or describe the meaning or significance of something

Support: provide evidence to back up or to prove your main idea

After you have an idea of what the general task is for your essay, look over each of the documents that follow. As you look at each document, ask yourself the **reporter's questions:** *who? what? when? where? why?* and *how?*

Who is pictured in the document? **Who** wrote or created it? **Whom** is it about? **Who** was its original audience?

What is the document about? **What** kind of document is it? **What** is the purpose of the document?

When and **where** was the document produced?

Why was the document made?

How does the document relate to its era?

Pay close attention to any **titles** and **captions,** or accompanying notes that appear with the documents. As you study the documents, take notes about them on scratch paper. Do not use complete sentences in your notes. Use phrases instead.

After you have studied the documents, answer each of the scaffolding questions. Use complete sentences in your answers. By answering these questions, you will gather information that you will be able to use in your essay.

Once you are finished with the scaffolding questions, you can begin work on your essay. Reread the essay question, and on your scratch paper write a one-sentence answer. This will become the thesis statement, or main idea, of your essay. Next, study the documents and your scaffolding question answers once again to find evidence. (For more information about essay writing, see Unit 3, starting on page 79.)

Exercise: Thinking about DBQs

1. What is a DBQ?

_____

_____

2. What are some kinds of documents?

_____

_____

3. What is the difference between a primary source and a secondary source?

_____

_____

4. What is a scaffolding question?

_____

_____

5. What is an essay question?

_____

_____

6. What kinds of questions should a person ask himself or herself when studying documents in on a DBQ test?

_____

_____

LESSON 2.1: STRATEGIES FOR ANALYZING PHOTOGRAPHS AND ILLUSTRATIONS

Understanding Photographs and Illustrations

People sometimes say, "A picture is worth a thousand words." What they mean is that a picture can contain lots of information. Two kinds of pictures that can show what life was like in the past are photographs and illustrations. An **illustration** is a work of art created to be printed, usually in a book, magazine, or newspaper. Types of illustrations include paintings, drawings, engravings, sketches, and cartoons. Illustrations can be created using any of a wide variety of materials from charcoal to paint.

A **photograph** is a print created from a piece of photographic film. Photography has been around since the 1800s. Before that time, people had to depend on illustrations and other artwork to record images of people and events.

When looking at photographs and illustrations, it is important to remember that there is a difference between just looking and really seeing. Take the time to study the details in the image. Ask yourself, "What does the picture tell me about the people and place in it?" Let's see how one student studied the photo below.

One Student's Response

Margaret Bourke-White was a photojournalist. At the end of World War II, she took this photograph of survivors of the concentration camp at Buchenwald. The survivors are wearing the striped uniforms of camp prisoners.

1. What does the photograph tell you about the treatment of people in the concentration camp?

After Cecelia read the question, she knew she had to look for specific information in the photograph. She had to search for clues about how the people in the photograph had been treated. She said to herself, "I'll look for words near the photo. Then I'll look at different parts of the photograph." First, she read the caption, the words near the photo that tell what it is about. The **caption** told her that the photo was of survivors of the Buchenwald concentration camp on the day they were liberated.

Next, Cecelia looked at the picture for clues. She noticed right away the power of the photograph: the stark look of despair in the people, how thin they were, their striped camp uniforms.

By noticing all these things, Cecelia gathered enough information to answer the question. She wrote, "The camp inmates endured terrible conditions and look exhausted but fiercely determined to stay alive." Then she checked her answer by rereading it and the question.

What to Look for in Photographs and Illustrations

Cecelia's answer shows how much information can be found in a document. There are some specific facts you should usually look for when studying pictures.

Title or Caption

When examining a photograph or illustration, you should begin by reading the title or caption. Doing so will probably give you some information about what is going on in the picture and about the era it is from.

Subject

The **subject** of any picture is very important. The subject is what the picture is of, such as a person or an animal. What does the subject look like? What is the subject wearing? Does the subject look happy? By studying how a person or thing looks, you can learn a lot. For example, if the people in a photograph are dressed in ragged clothes, you can guess they are not wealthy. Such an informed guess based on facts is called an **inference**.

Actions

Next, look to see what the subject is doing. Is there a specific activity, or **action,** occurring, or is the person or subject posing? The camp survivors in the Buchenwald photo are looking at the photographer.

Objects

Objects are the items in a picture that are not the main subject. For example, in the Buchenwald photo, the man at the right of the photo is holding a cane at an angle. By studying objects in a photo you can learn a lot about the activities or characteristics of the main subject. If a woman in a photograph is sitting near a table with china plates and silver utensils, you might guess that she was more likely to be rich than poor. Again, such an educated guess is called an inference.

Surroundings

Surroundings are what is around the subject(s) of the picture. Buildings, mountains, a large room—all are examples of surroundings. In the Buchenwald photograph, the background is dark so you can't see much of the surroundings, but the barbed wire in the foreground gives you a lot of information about the location and subject of the photograph. You can make inferences from surroundings, too. Even without a caption, seeing the barbed wire in the photo would tell you that the men in the picture were in some kind of restricted place.

How to Answer a Scaffolding Question about a Photograph or Illustration

Once you have studied a picture and thought about its parts, you can use the information you have gathered to answer the scaffolding question. You may have to put several clues together to draw a conclusion about how to respond to the question. By noticing the exhausted looks and the clothing of the subjects of the Buchenwald photograph, Cecelia made an inference, or informed guess, that the subjects had endured terrible conditions.

Even though you may have learned about several subjects, be sure that your response contains only the information requested. Make sure your answer is clear and shows that you understand how to **analyze,** or study, the document. To do that, state your opinion and then support it with evidence you have found in the document.

Strategy Review: Photographs and Illustrations

- Figure out what the question is asking.
- Use your own knowledge of history to help you interpret the picture.
- Study the title, caption, subject, objects, action, and surroundings in each image.
- Notice details in the picture, and make inferences based on these details.
- Answer the question clearly. In your answer, include one or two specific details from the picture.
- Reread your response to make sure you answered the question.

Remember: An **inference** is an informed, educated guess based on details that you have observed. For *all* documents, not just photographs and illustrations, develop the habit of making inferences about them on your own. The whole secret to understanding historical documents is to study them closely, notice the details, and then ask yourself, "What conclusions can I draw based on what I have observed?"

Exercise A: Thinking about Photographs and Illustrations

Directions:

Use the strategies you just learned to analyze the photograph below. You will answer the following scaffolding question at the end of the exercise: What is the relationship between the man who is seated and those around him?

A British gentleman in India having his feet manicured

1. In your own words, what does the question ask?

_____

_____

Take notes about the photograph.

2. What information does the caption give you?

_____

_____

3. Describe the subjects in the picture.

_____

_____

_____

4. What is happening in the photograph?

_____

_____

_____

5. Describe the objects in the photograph.

_____

_____

_____

6. What are the surroundings?

_____

_____

_____

7. **Answer the scaffolding question:** What is the relationship between the man who is seated and those around him?

_____

_____

_____

Exercise B. Scaffolding Question Practice: Photographs and Illustrations

Directions:

Answer the question that follows each photograph or illustration. Use strategies from the lesson to analyze the documents.

The English painter Thomas Baines traveled to Africa with the famed explorer David Livingstone in 1858.

1. In what way does this painting show a juxtaposition or encounter between two very different worlds?

_____

_____

_____

David Livingstone was a British missionary and explorer in Africa. When he hadn't been heard from for several years, people became worried about his safety. An American newspaper reporter, Henry M. Stanley, led a search for Livingstone. When he found Livingstone in 1871, Stanley greeted him with the following words, "Dr. Livingstone, I presume?"

2. What action do you see in the illustration?

_____

_____

The picture shows members of the Conservative Party Cabinet, including Benjamin Disraeli, circa 1876.

3. What does this picture suggest about the political rulers in Victorian England?

_____

_____

This photograph shows the funeral procession of Queen Victoria. King Edward VII is on the lead horse, followed by the German Kaiser Wilhelm II.

4. Queen Victoria ruled during the height of the British Empire, from 1837 to 1901. What information is given in the caption that provides a contrast with political funerals today in the United States?

LESSON 2.2: STRATEGIES FOR ANALYZING ADVERTISEMENTS AND POSTERS

Understanding Advertisements and Posters

Advertisements and posters are documents that are used to convince people to buy or do something. An **advertisement** often shows a product or event and lists its good qualities so people will buy or attend it or at least find out more about it. Advertisements appear in many different places, from magazines and newspapers to billboards. A **poster** is a large printed paper made for display purposes. It might be an advertisement for a product or event. It might contain information about a meeting or a situation that its creators want the public to know about.

Advertisements and posters can reveal a lot about their era by showing the products, events, and issues in which people were interested. For instance, an advertisement from the 1800s might picture a bottle of some questionable elixir (see page 30) and list its healing properties. That advertisement gives us information about the state of health care in that era. In order to get information from advertisements and posters, you must study them carefully.

The farm equipment business was very competitive in the 1800s. Inventors came up with new innovations that made the previous year's model seem obsolete. Companies frequently sued each other for stealing each other's patents.

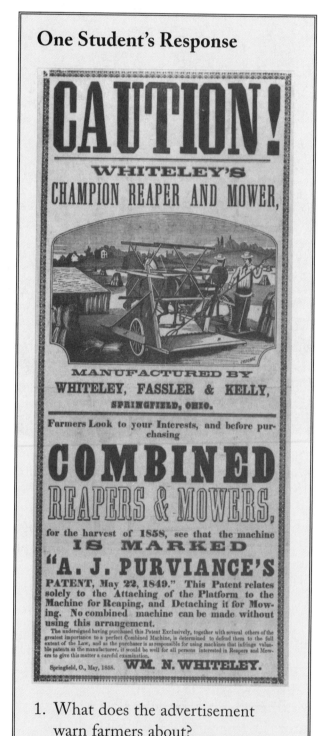

One Student's Response

1. What does the advertisement warn farmers about?

Orlando read the question and saw that he needed to read the ad closely to find the answer. First, he read the caption so that he would know what the ad was about. Then he read the text warning farmers to make sure that the machine they were considering purchasing was marked "A.J. Purviance's Patent, May 22, 1849." Orlando figured out that the ad was warning farmers that Whiteley's was the only legitimate machine to buy and that any other should be regarded as an inferior imitation. Orlando wrote his answer: "The ad warns farmers that Whiteley's makes the only legitimate combined reaper and mower."

What to Look for in Advertisements and Posters

When studying ads and posters, begin by thinking about the questions *who? what? when? where? and why?* After looking at the poster or ad, think about *what* you see in it. If it contains pictures, what do they show? In an ad, the picture may show a product or people using a product. These pictures represent life during a certain time and draw attention to the ad or poster.

Another important factor in determining what the poster is about is its text. Often, advertisements and posters contain several groups of words called **copy**. Groups of words might be printed in different sizes or typefaces. Usually, there is at least one **heading**, or line of text that is very large. The heading's purpose is to grab the viewer's attention so he or she will read the rest of the poster or ad. The heading might be a **slogan**, or phrase that is associated with the product or cause. The rest of the words in the document usually give specific information about the product or event. In the ad on page 28, the heading is "CAUTION!" Because that didn't tell Orlando anything specific, he read the smaller type below it to determine the ad's purpose and content.

After you have studied what is in a poster or ad, think about for *whom* it was made and *why*. In other words, think about the **audience** (at whom it was directed) and the **purpose** (why it was made and what response the creator of the piece wanted from the audience).

The audience of the ad on the previous page was obviously farmers. The ad's purpose was to convince farmers to buy Whiteley's Reaper and Mower, not a competitor's product.

Finally, try to determine *where* and *when* the ad or poster was created. Sometimes you must assemble clues and make an inference about where and when the ad or poster was produced. In this case, the specific answers to those questions are right in the ad: *Springfield, Ohio* and *1858*.

How to Answer a Scaffolding Question about an Advertisement or Poster

A question about a poster or advertisement may ask about its purpose, or how its different parts, such as the image, copy, heading, and slogan, work together. Read the question carefully and follow the steps in the strategy box below. Before you answer the question, review the notes you took while analyzing the ad or poster. Then write your answer.

Strategy Review: Advertisements and Posters

- Figure out what the question is asking.
- Look at the pictures.
- Look for headings or large type.
- Read the copy. Watch for slogans and think about what they tell you about the ad or poster.
- Think about the audience, the people for whom the ad or poster was made.
- Ask yourself why the ad or poster was made, or what its purpose was.
- Answer the question.

Exercise A: Thinking about Advertisements and Posters

Directions:

Use the strategies you just learned to analyze the advertisement on the right. You will answer the following scaffolding question at the end of the exercise: What does this advertisement want people to do?

1. In your own words, what does the question ask?

_____

_____

_____

_____

An advertisement for a cure for rheumatism.

Take notes about the advertisement.

2. What is happening in the picture?

_____

_____

_____

3. What is the caption?

_____

_____

_____

4. What does the copy claim the product will cure?

_____

_____

_____

5. Where can you buy this product?

_____

_____

_____

6. **Answer the scaffolding question:** What does this advertisement want people to do?

_____

_____

_____

Exercise B. Scaffolding Question Practice: Advertisements and Posters

Directions:

Answer the question that follows each advertisement or poster. Use the strategies from the lesson to analyze the documents.

L E S S O N   2 . 2

A White Star Line poster

1. To what two U.S. ports did the White Star ships go?

_____

_____

A 1925 poster printed in Zagreb for International Harvester Co. (Chicago)

2. What product is featured on this Polish poster?

_____

_____

A railroad advertisement offering service between Burlington, Vermont, and New York City

3. To what group of travelers does this advertisement appeal?

_____

_____

_____

This advertisement appeared in *Harper's Weekly*, an American magazine, in 1872.

4. What audiences does the manufacturer hope to reach with this advertisement?

_____

_____

_____

MINI-DBQ: EXERCISE

Exercise A: Analyzing Sources

Directions:

Answer the questions that follow each document.

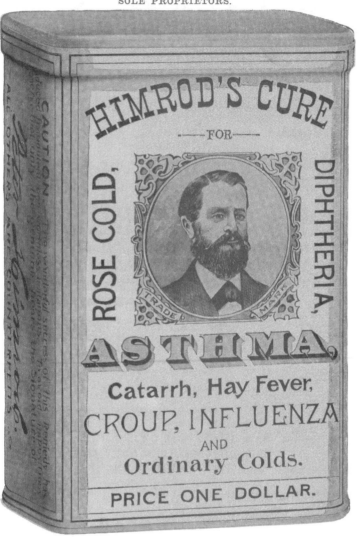

A 1895 advertisement for medicine

1. What does this product claim to do?

_____

_____

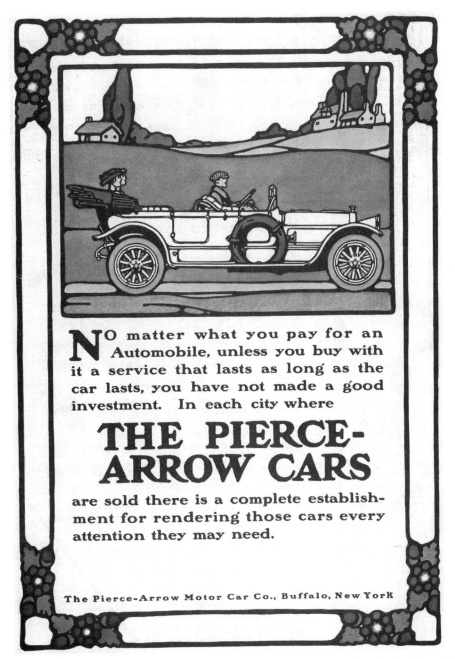

An advertisement for the Pierce-Arrow Motor Car Co., of Buffalo, New York

2. What action is taking place in the advertisement? How does the action help you to identify the target audience?

_____

_____

_____

Exercise B: Writing about Related Sources

Directions:

Write a paragraph in response to the long-answer question below. Be sure to include in your answer at least two details from documents on the previous pages. Reviewing your responses to scaffolding questions will help you to answer the long-answer question.

Long-answer question: How important was truth or factual accuracy in advertising claims during the Industrial Revolution?

_____

_____

_____

_____

_____

_____

_____

_____

_____

_____

_____

_____

_____

_____

_____

_____

MINI-DBQ

LESSON 2.3: STRATEGIES FOR ANALYZING POLITICAL CARTOONS

Understanding Political Cartoons

A **cartoon** is a humorous illustration. You are probably familiar with the ones that appear in the color cartoon sections of Sunday newspapers. Another kind is the **political cartoon**, which is a humorous illustration that makes a point about a political event or issue. Political cartoons often appear in magazines and on the editorial pages of newspapers. The cartoonist usually includes more than just the facts and exaggerates parts of the drawing to emphasize his or her opinion.

For example, to show that a candidate is backed by big business, a political cartoon might show a sneaky-looking candidate taking money out of the pocket of a portly character labeled "Big Business."

Cartoons often contain **symbols,** or pictures that stand for something else. For instance, a bald eagle can serve as a symbol of the American government. Studying political cartoons can teach us about the problems and issues that were important during a particular time.

One Student's Response

Theodore Roosevelt shovels dirt from the Panama Canal onto Bogotá, Colombia, after the U.S. supports Panama's revolution for independence in exchange for U.S. control of the Panama Canal Zone.

1. What is the message of this cartoon?

After reading the question, Katie looked at the cartoon. "Who is the guy with the shovel?" was the first thought that occurred to her. She read the caption, which told her that the main character was President Theodore Roosevelt. She studied the caption more closely and looked at the cartoon.

Then she understood that Roosevelt's dirt was dropping on Bogotá, the capital of Colombia. Reading carefully, and remembering her history, Katie realized the main message of the cartoon. Panama had been part of Colombia. The United States had offered to buy a part of Panama from Colombia, but Colombia refused the deal. So with American help, people in Panama organized a revolution and declared independence. Then they quickly gave the Canal Zone to the United States so construction of the canal could begin. "Aha!" thought Katie, "that explains the little guy up there with the flag saying 'New Treaty.'" It's a symbol for the Colombian government.

So what is the message of the cartoon? Katie wrote, "The cartoonist seems to disapprove of Roosevelt's action. He makes Roosevelt look gigantic to symbolize American power. And the Colombians are the victims."

What to Look for in Political Cartoons

Images and Symbols

The **images,** or pictures, in a political cartoon are very important because they show the subjects with which the cartoonist was concerned. Each image usually represents, or is a **symbol** of, something else. A particular image might stand for a person, a country, an organization, or an idea. For example, when Teddy Roosevelt was president, teddy bears were often used in cartoons to represent the president.

Labels

Often, to help viewers understand what the parts of a political cartoon symbolize, the cartoonist uses labels. **Labels** are words or abbreviations that tell what an item in a picture is supposed to represent. In the cartoon on page 39, the label "New Treaty" helped Katie to understand the cartoon.

Captions

Sometimes political cartoons include **captions**—words or phrases that appear above, below, or within the cartoon and provide information about it. In the case of the cartoon on page 39, the caption contains a wealth of information.

Speech

Sometimes political cartoons include words or phrases that characters in the cartoons are supposed to be saying.

Message

The **message** is the cartoonist's opinion about an issue, person, place, or event. The message is communicated by the combination of images and words in the cartoon. You can understand the message by thinking about what the text and pictures mean together. Ask yourself, "What issue or event is this cartoon about?" and "What is the cartoonist's opinion about this issue or event?"

How to Answer a Scaffolding Question about a Political Cartoon

A scaffolding question about a political cartoon will usually ask you about the cartoon's overall message. You will not be able to figure out the cartoon's message without studying the words and pictures first. Read the question carefully, then follow the steps in the box below. Be sure to answer the whole question.

Strategy Review: Political Cartoons

- Figure out what the question is asking.
- Figure out what all the items in the picture symbolize. Pay attention to labels that tell you what the items stand for.
- Read any captions or speech bubbles that are part of the cartoon.
- Ask yourself what issue or event the cartoon is about.
- Figure out the cartoonist's opinion or overall message.
- Answer the question.

Exercise A: Thinking about Political Cartoons

Directions:

Use the strategies you have just learned to analyze the cartoon below. You will answer the following scaffolding question at the end of the exercise: What is the message of this cartoon?

Dame Europa: "To whom do I owe the pleasure of this intrusion?

Uncle Sam: "Ma'am, my name is Uncle Sam!"

Dame Europa: "Any relation to the late Colonel Monroe?"

The reference to Colonel Monroe is a reference to President James Monroe. In the Monroe Doctrine, the U.S. pledged to stay out of European affairs. Until the Spanish-American War, the U.S. had honored its promise to Europe.

Take notes about the political cartoon.

1. Whom do the two figures in the cartoon represent?

_____

_____

_____

2. What meaning can you infer from how the two figures in the cartoon are standing?

_____

_____

_____

3. What information in the dialogue reinforces the meaning you inferred from how the two figures in the cartoon are standing?

_____

_____

_____

4. What is the symbolism of the stripes on the pants of the male figure?

_____

_____

_____

5. What prediction is the cartoonist making about the United States' involvement in Europe?

_____

_____

_____

6. **Answer the scaffolding question:** What is the message of this cartoon?

_____

_____

_____

Understanding Political Cartoons: Images and Symbols

The Rhodes Colossus Standing from Cape Town to Cairo

In this political cartoon, there are several images:

1. A European man
2. A map of Africa
3. A man holding telegraph wires spanning the continent.

Cecil Rhodes (1853–1902) was a British businessman who became prime minister of the British colony of South Africa. The cartoonist is referring to Rhodes as one of the seven wonders of the ancient world. The harbor of the Greek island of Rhodes was guarded by a colossal statue of the sun god, Helios, that spanned the opening of the harbor.

A political cartoon is created to express the cartoonist's opinion. What is this cartoonist suggesting about Cecil Rhodes' ambitions in Africa?

Exercise B. Scaffolding Question Practice: Political Cartoons

Answer the question that follows each cartoon. Use the strategies from the lesson to analyze the documents.

The Belgian colonization of the Congo was particularly brutal. Belgian officials tortured and murdered Africans. King Leopold denied all claims of mistreatment, but then was confronted with photographic evidence. This was an early example of photojournalism being used to prove official misconduct.

1. How does the cartoonist view King Leopold?

_____

_____

_____

PUCK.

SPANISH MISRULE

ANARCHY

THE DUTY OF THE HOUR:—TO SAVE HER NOT ONLY FROM SPAIN BUT FROM A WORSE FATE.

In the 1890s, Cuban revolutionaries began an uprising in Cuba against Spanish rule.

2. What does the woman in the skillet symbolize?

_____

_____

_____

Chamberlain: "The lowest corner down yonder, must be painted red!"

Following Chamberlain's directions, Queen Victoria paints South Africa red with blood. This cartoon appeared in a German newspaper. Germany sided with Dutch settlers in the Boer War.

3. What does the cartoonist think of British actions in South Africa?

_____

_____

_____

In 1857, Indian troops revolted against their British officers in India. The British put down the rebellion with such force and bloodshed that some British officers protested. Note: The lion was a traditional symbol of the British Empire. The tiger was a traditional symbol of India.

4. What do you think the cartoonist was trying to express in this cartoon?

_____

_____

_____

LESSON 2.4: STRATEGIES FOR ANALYZING INFORMATIONAL GRAPHICS

Understanding Informational Graphics

A **graphic** is a special kind of illustration that presents facts, or information. If you've ever looked at an atlas or made a graph in math class, you've worked with an informational graphic. There are many different kinds of **informational graphics**, including maps, bar graphs, pie charts, charts, diagrams, and time lines.

Informational graphics serve many different purposes. For instance, a battlefield map would show the positions of the opposing armies. A time line might show the order of events before, during, and after the battle. A pie chart might show the percent of troops in each army. A graph might compare the number of casualties in one battle with casualties in another battle.

One Student's Response

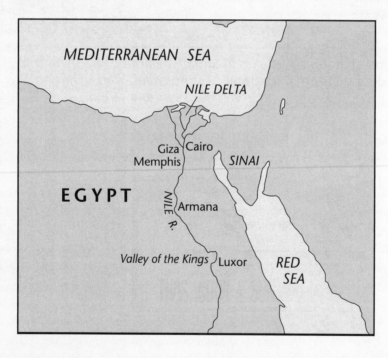

This map shows the civilization of Ancient Egypt that flourished along the Nile River.

1. What was the main transportation route in ancient Egypt?

Alicia read the question and looked at the map. At first she was puzzled. She had expected to see a map key that explained different transportation routes. Instead, all she saw was the map, the Nile River, and the cities along the river. Alicia told herself not to panic—she could figure this out. She looked over the entire map. The only information she saw was the names of cities, the location of the Nile River, and other bodies of water—the Mediterranean Sea and the Red Sea. The answer quickly became apparent to Alicia. She wrote: "The map shows that the main transportation route was the Nile River."

What to Look for in Informational Graphics

Title

The title of an informational graphic can tell about its subject or purpose and usually tells what era the information is from.

Headings and Labels

Some informational graphics, like bar graphs, also have labels or headings that give more specific information about the facts presented. Maps sometimes have a **compass rose** that shows directions. A map may also have **legend** or a **key** that explains symbols used on it or a scale that shows how the distances on the map relate to actual distances.

Details

Some informational graphics contain a lot of information. It is important to notice all the details in the graphic. For instance, a **map** might show information about a specific location, the distances between different places, or the layout of a city. **Time lines** contain information about dates and the sequence in which events happened.

Reading Bar Graphs

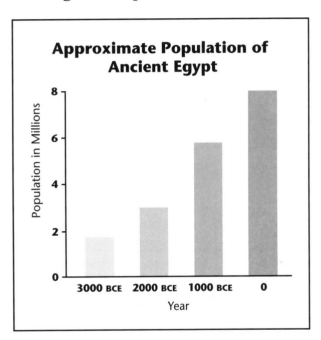

A **bar graph** presents information about two or more different items known as **variables**. The labels on the graph tell you what the variables are. In the bar graph above, the variables are years and number of people. You can read the bar graph shown above by starting at the top of one of the bars and running your finger across to the number on the left scale. Reading the graph you can see that in 2000 BCE there were about 3 million people living in Egypt.

Reading Pie Charts

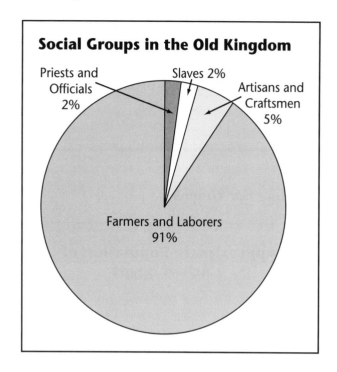

Social Groups in the Old Kingdom

Priests and Officials 2%

Slaves 2%

Artisans and Craftsmen 5%

Farmers and Laborers 91%

A **pie chart** is made using a circle to represent the whole amount. The sections of a pie chart show the parts of the whole. Pay attention to how each "slice" of the "pie" relates to the others. The pie chart here shows that about 2% of the population of Ancient Egypt was slaves.

How to Answer a Scaffolding Question about an Informational Graphic

For all informational graphics, make sure you carefully read the title and labels. For maps, study the legend or key, if there is one, and notice what items are represented on the map and their relationships to one another. For bar graphs, make sure to identify the two variables. For pie charts, pay attention to the parts and their relationship to the whole.

Strategy Review: Informational Graphics

• Make sure that you understand what the scaffolding question is asking you.
• Study the title or caption to find out the main idea of the graphic.
• Pay attention to details.
• Remember to look for values of the variables in bar graphs.
• Use the scale, compass rose, and legend to get valuable information about a map.
• Remember to compare the parts with the whole when studying a pie chart.
• Answer the whole question.
• Reread your answer to make sure it is correct.

Exercise A: Thinking about Informational Graphics

Directions:

Use the strategies you learned in this lesson to analyze the time line below. You will answer the following scaffolding question: During which kingdom did the construction of the great pyramids begin?

Kingdoms of Ancient Egypt

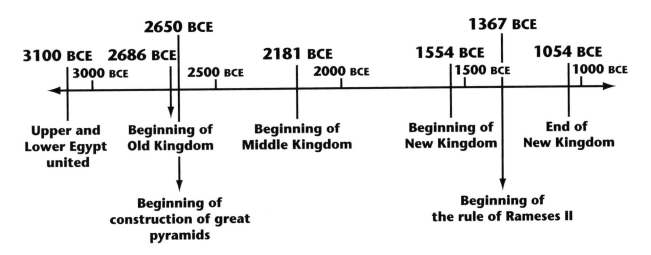

1. In your own words, what does the question ask?

_____

_____

Take notes about the informational graphic.

2. What is the title of the time line?

_____

_____

3. What is the graphic about?

_____

_____

4. List some details from the time line.

_____

_____

5. **Answer the scaffolding question:** During which kingdom did the construction of the great pyramids begin?

_____

_____

Exercise B. Scaffolding Question Practice: Informational Graphics

Directions:

Answer the question that follows each informational graphic. Use the strategies from the lesson to analyze the documents.

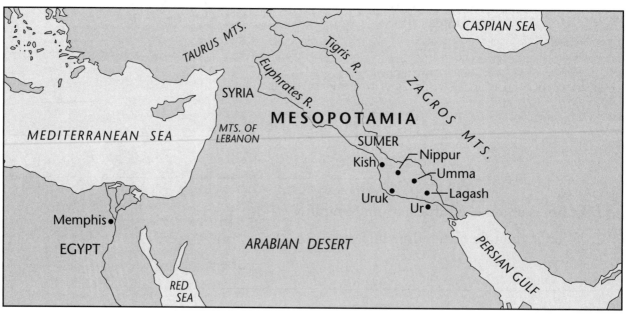

Ancient Mesopotamia

1. What two rivers created the fertile valley of Mesopotamia?

_____

_____

Time Line of Mesopotamia

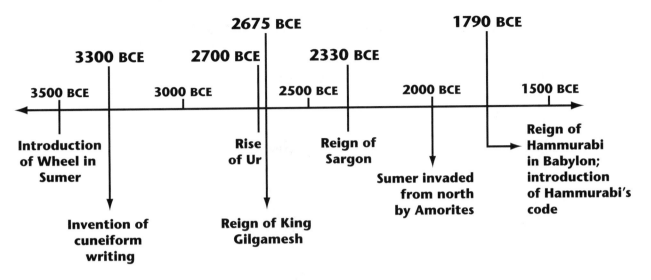

2. When was cuneiform writing invented?

_____

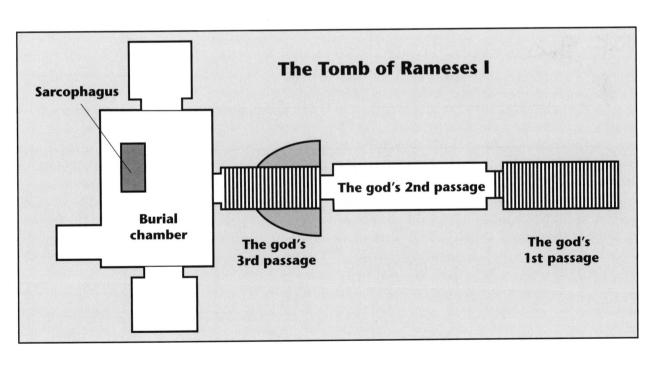

3. What is the name of the steps nearest the sarcophagus?

_____

Phoenician Alphabet

Sign	Meaning	Latin	Sign	Meaning	Latin
⪤	Ox	A	⪫	?	E
⪦	House	B	⪎	?	F
⪧	Camel	C, G	⪣	Wall	H
△	Door	D	⪜	Hand	I, J

4. Use the chart to identify the Phoenician meaning of the following:

⪤ ⪦ △

_____

_____

LESSON 2.5: STRATEGIES FOR ANALYZING LETTERS AND EYEWITNESS ACCOUNTS

Understanding Letters and Eyewitness Accounts

Most **letters** are private messages written from one person to another. Sometimes, however, people write letters meant to be published for a wide audience, such as **letters to the editor** of a newspaper. Historians are interested in letters because they reveal a lot about the values, beliefs, experiences, and feelings of people who lived in the past. An **eyewitness account** is a document that is written or spoken by someone who saw or took part in an event. Diaries, journals, police reports, court transcripts, and interviews are all eyewitness accounts.

When reading letters and eyewitness accounts, be careful to distinguish facts from opinions. A **fact** is a statement that can be proven true. An **opinion** is a statement from an individual's point of view—his or her beliefs, desires, or judgments. Accounts of the same event written by two different people might be very different. For example, the immigration experience of a Chinese immigrant who faced discrimination in 1940 would be very different from the immigration experience of a Northern European immigrant in 1870. Read below how Jamil analyzed the letter by an English traveler commenting on American immigration laws.

One Student's Response

The month of May 1881 was marked by the most extraordinary anomaly which could possibly have arisen, among a people whose national existence is based on the Declaration of Independence, and the assumption of liberty and equality of all men, without distinction of race or colour.

This extraordinary event was nothing less than that the American Legislature should have yielded to the clamours of the low Irish in California, and to their ceaseless anti-Chinese howl, to the extent of actually passing a law prohibiting all Chinese immigration for the next ten years.

Constance Gordon-Cumming (1837–1924) was an astute observer of local customs and wrote many letters. In the letter excerpted above, Ms. Gordon-Cumming further explained that the agitation that led to the restrictions on Chinese immigration was related to competition for jobs.

1. At one point in her letter, after the excerpt that appears above, Ms. Gordon-Cumming refers to the anti-immigration legislation as "utterly un-American." Given what she said in the excerpt, why might she consider such legislation un-American?

Jamil read the question and the entry carefully. He noticed that in the entry, Ms. Gordon-Cumming expressed surprise that such legislation would be passed "among a people whose national existence is based on the Declaration of Independence." Jamil wrote the following response: "Ms. Gordon-Cumming, though obviously not free of prejudice herself, seems to have felt that the restriction on Chinese immigration unfairly singled out one race of people, which was in direct contradiction to the 'assumption of liberty and equality of all men' found in the Declaration of Independence on which the country was based."

What to Look for in Letters and Eyewitness Accounts

Caption

Although most of your information will come from the account itself, the caption might give some background information about the eyewitness or event.

Speaker

Knowing the identity of the eyewitness might tell you whether the account is reliable. For instance, the eyewitness testimony of a Nazi concentration camp guard about the conditions in the camp could not be considered reliable, because of his point of view. People often perceive issues and events differently based on their beliefs and interests.

Purpose

Knowing the type of eyewitness account will also help you to interpret it. For instance, a diary entry is more likely to reveal truths than a letter written to sell a product.

Setting

Ask yourself where and when the event took place. This information is important because it tells you about the time and place of the event, two facts that may help you form an opinion of the speaker.

Main Idea

The **main idea** is what the account is mostly about. The main idea of an eyewitness account of a battle would probably be the events and result of the battle.

Details

The **details** in a paragraph are the pieces of information that support the main idea. For instance, two details that might support the main idea that a battle was poorly waged might be the poor positioning of troops and the failure to coordinate an attack.

How to Answer a Scaffolding Question about a Letter or Eyewitness Account

After reading a letter or eyewitness account, take notes on it. Think about how the speaker, setting, and main idea work together. For instance, a first-hand account of the Battle of the Marne written by someone who fought in it is more valuable

Strategy Review: Letters and Eyewitness Accounts

- Figure out what the question is asking.
- Look for background and setting information in the caption.
- Think about the person giving the account. Ask yourself, "Who is writing what to whom?" Think about whether the writer seems reliable.
- Think about the purpose of the account and how it affects the message.
- Make sure you understand the main idea or message.
- Read the account carefully and record details that support the main idea.
- Answer the whole question.

than an account by the soldier's parents, who learned about it in a letter from their son, and either is more valuable than a third-hand account by someone who learned about it by hearing the parents talk about the letter.

Exercise A: Thinking about Letters and Eyewitness Accounts

Directions:

Use the strategies you have just learned to analyze the eyewitness account below. You will answer the following scaffolding question at the end of the exercise: How did the opportunity to play baseball change Wilma Briggs's life?

In 1995, an honors English class in Rhode Island conducted a research program titled "What did you do in the war, Grandma?" The students interviewed Rhode Island women about their experiences during World War II. What follows is an excerpt from an interview with Wilma Briggs, a professional baseball player.

Had it not been for the war, that part of my life would never have come to pass. And I think because I went out there and played ball—I met a lot of people from all over the United States, Canada, and Cuba, which I never would have done. I traveled, lived in the best hotels, ate in restaurants, lived in private homes—that's an experience. I think it gave me the courage years later to say, "I think I'll go to college." The league ended finally in '54. All those things that people couldn't do during the war years they could now do. They had money in their pockets, gasoline in their gas tanks, and television came out. I think that's what broke the back of that league. People could do so much more after the war.

---

1. In your own words, what does the question ask?

_____

_____

_____

Take notes about the eyewitness account.

2. According to the caption, what type of eyewitness account are you reading?

_____

_____

_____

3. What is the main idea?

_____

_____

_____

4. List details that support the main idea.

_____

_____

_____

5. Why did the baseball league end?

_____

_____

_____

6. **Answer the scaffolding question:** How did the opportunity to play baseball change Wilma Briggs's life?

_____

_____

_____

Exercise B. Scaffolding Question Practice: Letters and Eyewitness Accounts

Answer the question that follows each letter or eyewitness account. Use the strategies from the lesson to analyze the documents.

In 399 BCE, the Greek philosopher Socrates was condemned to drink poison, allegedly for impiety and corrupting the youth of Athens. The following is a selection from an eyewitness account of Socrates' death.

> *I covered my face and wept broken-heartedly — not for him, but for my own calamity in losing such a friend… Apollodorus… now broke out in such a storm of passionate weeping that he made everyone in the room break down, except Socrates himself, who said: "Really, my friends, what a way to behave!…I am told that one should make one's end in a reverent silence. Calm yourselves and be brave."*

Excerpt from Plato's *Phaedo*

1. According to Socrates, how should a person meet his death?

_____

_____

This diary was written by Ginger, a 17-year-old girl who lived at Hickam Air Field with her family.

> *Sunday, December 7, 1941*
>
> *BOMBED! 8:00 in the morning. Unknown attacker so far! Pearl Harbor in flames!…*
>
> *11:05. We've left the post. It got too hot. The PX [Post Exchange] is in flames, also the barracks. We made a dash during a lull. Left everything we own there. Found out the attackers are Japanese. Rats!!! A couple of non-com's [non-commissioned officers] houses demolished.*

2. What first-hand information does the writer report?

_____

_____

_____

Anne Frank wrote these observations in her diary on January 13, 1943.

> *Terrible things are happening outside. At anytime of night and day, poor helpless people are dragged out of their homes…Families are torn apart…As for us, we're quite fortunate. Luckier than millions of people…I could spend hours telling you about the suffering the war has brought, but I'd only make myself more miserable. All we can do is wait, as calmly as possible, for it to end. Jews and Christians alike are waiting, the whole world is waiting, and many are waiting for death.*

3. What event that Anne has observed prompts her thoughts in this diary entry?

_____

_____

_____

Elizabeth Bayley Willis taught art, Latin, and English at Garfield High School in Seattle. In 1942, many of her Japanese-American students were sent away to internment camps. Mrs. Willis sent the students supplies and kept up a correspondence with them. The letter below is from a high school girl.

> *What I wouldn't give to be back in Seattle next September to continue my studies at Garfield. Many of the boys say this too. Some of them who were not good students and didn't like school even say this. It is my belief that everyone here would like to go back to their normal life.*
> *But recently I've read quite a bit about taking away the U.S. citizenship of the American born Japanese and to deport them after the war. The Native Sons and Daughters of the Golden West are trying to do this, and from what I read they are in dead earnest. Our citizenship is very dear to us and I hope this thing never occurs.*

4. What fear does the writer communicate to Mrs. Willis?

_____

_____

_____

MINI-DBQ: THE BIRTH OF NUCLEAR WEAPONS

Exercise A: Analyzing Sources

Directions:

Answer the question that follows each document.

In August of 1939, at the urging of fellow physicists, Albert Einstein wrote to President Roosevelt to warn that the Germans might be working on nuclear weapons and to urge Roosevelt to begin his own research program. The Manhattan Project, born of this letter, produced the first nuclear weapon, which was exploded at the Trinity test site in Alamogordo, New Mexico, in July of 1945.

In the course of the last four months it has been made probable—through the work of Joliet in France as well as Fermi and Szilard in America—that it may become possible to set up a nuclear chain reaction in a large mass of uranium, by which vast amounts of power and large quantities of new radium-like elements would be generated. Now it appears almost certain that this could be achieved in the immediate future.

This new phenomenon would also lead to the construction of bombs, and it is conceivable —though much less certain—that extremely powerful bombs of a new type may thus be constructed. A single bomb of this type, carried by boat and exploded in a port, might very well destroy the whole port together with some of the surrounding territory.

Letter from Albert Einstein to President Franklin Delano Roosevelt, August 2, 1939

1. What did Einstein warn President Roosevelt about in the letter written in 1939?

_____

_____

On the morning of the 16th of July, I was stationed at the Base Camp at Trinity in a position about ten miles from the site of the explosion. The explosion took place at about 5:30 A.M. I had my face protected by a large board in which a piece of dark welding glass had been inserted. My first impression of the explosion was the very intense flash of light, and a sensation of heat on the parts of my body that were exposed. Although I did not look directly towards the object, I had the impression that suddenly the countryside became brighter than

---

> *in full daylight. I subsequently looked in the direction of the explosion through the dark glass and could see something that looked like a conglomeration of flames that promptly started rising. After a few seconds the rising flames lost their brightness and appeared as a huge pillar of smoke with an expanded head like a gigantic mushroom that rose rapidly beyond the clouds probably to a height of 30,000 feet. After reaching its full height, the smoke stayed stationary for a while before the wind started dissipating it.*
>
> *About 40 seconds after the explosion the air blast reached me. I tried to estimate its strength by dropping from about six feet small pieces of paper before, during, and after the passage of the blast wave. Since, at the time, there was no wind I could observe very distinctly and actually measure the displacement of the pieces of paper that were in the process of falling while the blast was passing. The shift was about 2 1/2 meters, which, at the time, I estimated to correspond to the blast that would be produced by ten thousand tons of T.N.T.*

Eyewitness account by physicist Enrico Fermi of the first nuclear test at the Trinity site in New Mexico, July 16, 1945

2. What did the first nuclear explosion look like? How powerful did the physicist Enrico Fermi estimate the explosion to be?

_____

_____

> *"On July 24 I casually mentioned to Stalin that we had a new weapon of unusual destructive force. The Russian Premier showed no special interest. All he said was that he was glad to hear it and hoped we would make 'good use of it against the Japanese.'"*

Excerpt from President Harry Truman's *Year of Decisions*

3. According to Truman, what was unusual about the nuclear bomb?

_____

_____

> *The fires must have receded. I was alive. My friends had somehow managed to rescue me....The entire northern side of the city was completely burned. The sky was still dark, but whether it was evening or midday I could not tell....The streets were deserted except for the dead. Some looked as if they had been frozen by death while in the full action of flight; others lay sprawled as though some giant had flung them to their death from a great height.*

Excerpt from Michihiko Hachiya's *Hiroshima Diary*

4. What effect did the nuclear explosion have on the city of Hiroshima, according to Hachiya's eyewitness account?

_____

_____

_____

Exercise B: Writing from Letters and Eyewitness Accounts

Directions:

Write a paragraph in response to the long-answer question below. Be sure to include in your answer at least four details taken from the documents that you have just studied. Reviewing your answers to the scaffolding question will help you to answer the long-answer question.

Long-answer question: How did the first nuclear weapons come into existence, and what was exceptional about them? Explain, drawing upon the documents in this lesson.

_____

_____

_____

_____

_____

MINI-DBQ

LESSON 2.6: STRATEGIES FOR ANALYZING NEWSPAPER AND MAGAZINE ARTICLES

Understanding Newspaper and Magazine Articles

Newspaper and magazine articles are usually written by professional journalists about current events. An eyewitness account tells only one person's view of an event. Newspaper and magazine articles are often based upon information gathered from several people and other sources. They usually contain facts that are generally agreed upon and reliable.

Articles are usually written to tell people facts about important recent events. For instance, people read the newspaper to find out if their favorite baseball team won or if Congress passed an important bill.

Newspaper and magazine articles can tell us a lot about historical events or issues. They can tell us what facts about an event were known to the writer at the time. Sometimes articles also include people's reactions or opinions.

When you read articles about unfamiliar places and people or about complicated issues, you may have some difficulty understanding them. At times you may need to reread an excerpt to understand its main idea. The main idea, of course, is the most important topic found in the excerpt.

One Student's Response

We came to the question: what to do with the women and children? I decided to find a clear solution here as well. I did not consider myself justified to exterminate the men—that is, to kill them or have them killed—and allow the avengers of our sons and grandsons in the form of their children to grow up. The difficult decision had to be [made] to make this people disappear from the earth.

Part of a speech by Nazi official Heinrich Himmler, October 6, 1943. Speech excerpts often appear in articles in newspapers of record like the *The Washington Post* or *The New York Times*. Newspapers of record have a reputation for accuracy and completeness that allow historians and researchers to rely on them.

1. How does Himmler justify the execution of women and children?

First Raul read the caption, which explained that the excerpt came from a speech by a Nazi official. Reading the excerpt, he noted that Himmler decided to exterminate Jewish men and then decided to kill women and children as well.

Raul also noted that Himmler's explanation was that the action was necessary to prevent revenge by future generations of Jews against Nazi descendants. Raul wrote, "Himmler justified a policy of killing not only Jewish men, but also Jewish women and children by saying that he wanted to prevent acts of revenge by Jews in the future."

What to Look for in Newspaper and Magazine Articles

Headlines, Titles, Headings, and Captions

A newspaper article almost always begins with a **headline** printed in bigger type than the article itself. The headline has two purposes: to grab the reader's attention and to tell what the main idea of the article is. The **title** that appears at the beginning of a magazine article serves the same purpose. Often a magazine article will also include subtitles, or **headings**, that appear throughout the article and tell what parts of the article are about. When a piece, or **excerpt**, of a newspaper or magazine article appears in a book or on a test, it often includes a **caption**—a few words that may identify the time, place, author, or subject of the excerpt. Headlines, titles, headings, and captions are useful because they can tell you what the main idea of a piece is.

The Five Ws

Often, reporters have to pack a lot of information into their articles. Reporters speak of the **five Ws**, *who, what, where, when,* and *why,* as the foundation upon which an article builds. *Who* is the subject of the article. It might be a person, thing, or event. *What* is the subject's action, or what the subject is doing. *Where* and *when* are the setting of the action—the location and time. *Why* can be the most challenging information to uncover. Sometimes an article will tell why something is happening. When it does not, you must draw conclusions based on your knowledge of the other four Ws. You may have to make an **inference**, or educated guess, about why something is happening, based on facts from the article and what you already know about the era.

Main Idea and Details

The **main idea** of an article is what it is mostly about. In an article, the main idea is supported by particular, specific facts that are known as **details**. For instance, the horrific main idea of the Himmler excerpt is that Jewish women and children will be part of the "Final Solution." A detail supporting the main idea is Himmler's fear of future acts of revenge.

How to Answer a Scaffolding Question about a Newspaper or Magazine Article

Read the question, paying close attention to key words that tell you what to do. Then read the article and take notes on the five Ws as you read. Next, think about the article's main idea. Finally, answer the question, using details from the document in your answer.

Strategy Review: Newspaper and Magazine Articles

- Figure out what the question is asking.
- Scan the article or excerpt, looking at headlines, titles, headings, and captions that will tell you what the main idea of the piece is.
- Read the article carefully. As you read, ask yourself how the article answers the questions *who? what? where? when?* and *why?*
- Think about what the main idea of the article is and how specific facts and other details relate to this main idea.
- Answer the question completely.

Exercise A: Thinking about Newspaper and Magazine Articles

Directions:

Use the strategies you just learned to analyze the magazine excerpt below. You will answer the following scaffolding question at the end of the exercise: What dilemma did the American government face as it began the war on terrorism?

> [T]he response from Muslims around the world, even those who reacted with glee at news of the attacks on the Pentagon and World Trade Center... and those of other Muslims who were either dismayed or disgusted by the promise of a U.S. military response, posed an enormous problem for American policymakers from the start... There seemed little reason to launch any kind of military action against [terrorist leader Osama] bin Laden's adopted homeland if it was only sure to split Bush's coalition, deepen foreign resentment of the U.S. —and leave bin Laden at large.

Excerpt from an article from *Time* magazine, October 15, 2001

1. In your own words, what does the question ask?

_____

_____

Take notes about the article.

2. What is the source of the article?

_____

3. When was the article written?

_____

4. Who or what is the subject of the article?

_____

_____

5. **Answer the scaffolding question:** What dilemma did the American government face as it began the war on terrorism?

_____

_____

_____

Exercise B. Scaffolding Question Practice: Newspaper and Magazine Articles

Directions:

Answer the question that follows each excerpt. Use the strategies from the lesson to analyze the documents.

Here's the truth: What radicalized the Sept. 11 terrorists was not that they suffered from a poverty of food, it was that they suffered from a poverty of dignity. Frustrated by the low standing of Muslim countries in the world, compared with Europe or the United States, and the low standing in which they were personally held where they were living [in Europe], they were easy pickings for militant preachers who knew how to direct their rage.

"Many of the terrorists we are now confronting are a Western phenomenon, existing inside the Islamic diaspora [out-migration] in the U.S. and Europe," wrote Adrian Karatnycky, the president of Freedom House…These men are not "sleepers" planted within Europe years in advance by bin Laden, he argues; instead, they are minted right there, when they encounter the West.

Excerpt from editorial in *The New York Times*, January 27, 2002

1. What opinion does the editorial express? What details are used to support that opinion?

_____

_____

_____

COALITION-BUILDING: U.S. Asks Rest of World to Join Terrorism Fight

By Edward Epstein
CHRONICLE WASHINGTON BUREAU

WASHINGTON—*The United States began yesterday building a broad international coalition to support and possibly join in military retaliation against those responsible for Tuesday's lethal attacks on New York and Washington, officials said.*

In a capital city where there are calls for President Bush to ask Congress to approve a formal declaration of war, Secretary of State

Colin Powell said the administration was mounting a "full-court press diplomatically, politically, militarily."

Defense Secretary Donald Rumsfeld told U.S. armed forces they would soon have the chance to be "heroes" in the "days ahead," hinting at a major military response soon.

"The task of vanquishing these terrible enemies—and protecting the American people and the cause of human freedom—will fall to you," he said.

San Francisco Chronicle, September 13, 2001

2. What is the main idea of the article?

_____

_____

_____

> PARIS—*European and other world leaders are firing public warning shots across Washington's bow, urgently seeking to forestall any move to make Iraq the next target in the US war on terrorists.*
>
> *"All European nations would view a widening of the conflict with great skepticism, and that is putting it diplomatically," German Foreign Minister Joschka Fischer told the Bundestag on Wednesday. It would be "irresponsible to look for new targets."*

The Christian Science Monitor, November 30, 2001

3. According to the article, what is Europe's position? Why?

_____

_____

> AZHAKHEL BALA, Pakistan, Jan. 20—*Little in the manner of Ijaz Khan Hussein betrays the miseries he saw as a volunteer in the war in Afghanistan.*
>
> *Mr. Khan, a college-trained pharmacist, joined the jihad, or holy war, like thousands of other Pakistanis who crossed over into Afghanistan. He worked as a medical orderly near Kabul, shuttling to the front lines....*
>
> *Now with the Taliban and Al Qaeda routed, have Mr. Khan and other militants finished with holy war?*
>
> *Mr. Khan, at least, said he had not.*
>
> *"We went to the jihad filled with joy, and I would go again tomorrow," he said. "If Allah had chosen me to die, I would have been in paradise, eating honey and watermelons and grapes, ...just as it is promised in the Koran. Instead, my fate was to remain amid the unhappiness here on earth."*
>
> *Jihad literally means striving. The Prophet Muhammad gave Muslims the task of striving in the path of God. Whether that striving is armed or a personal duty of conscience is a question causing consternation in the world's 1.2 billion Muslims, and that question goes to the heart of President Bush's war on terrorism.*

The New York Times, January 2002

4. What major challenge in the war on terrorism does this article highlight? What details support that point?

_____

_____

_____

LESSON 2.7: STRATEGIES FOR ANALYZING OFFICIAL GOVERNMENT DOCUMENTS

Understanding Official Government Documents

In the course of their operations, governments create a lot of documents. **Official government documents** include all the papers created by or filed with a government. Many of these documents, from the constitution that sets up a government to the laws that it passes, are **legal documents**—ones that are binding in court. Some government documents, such as speeches given by officials or proceedings of legislative bodies, are simply records of government activities. Often, to carry out normal activities, such as getting married, registering a car, or applying for a student loan, ordinary citizens have to file official documents with government agencies. Historians are interested in government documents because they reveal a lot about past events. The following chart describes some common government documents.

Agenda: A list of topics to be covered in a meeting, often including a list of participants

Bill: A draft of a law to be considered by a legislative body, such as a congress or parliament

Birth Certificate: A legal document giving a person's name, date of birth, and place of birth

Constitution: A document presenting the basic laws under which a government is formed

Decision: In law, a document giving a court's verdict in a case, usually including the reasoning behind the verdict

Declaration: A formal statement of intent or purpose, such as a declaration of war

Deed: A legal document showing ownership of a piece of real property such as land or a house

Judgment: In law, a ruling or verdict made by a court

Legislative Record/Proceedings: A regularly published series of documents describing the activities of a legislative body, including information on bills and resolutions considered, actions taken, records of meetings of committees and subcommittees, records of votes cast, transcripts of speeches and hearings, and other important data

Marriage Certificate: A legal document recording the date and place of a marriage and the names and signatures of the people who were married, of witnesses to the marriage, and of the official who performed the marriage ceremony

Marriage License: A legal document granting a couple the right to become married

Minutes: An official record of a meeting

Pardon: An official document forgiving an individual who has committed a crime

Proclamation: An official statement, issued by a monarch or by the chief executive officer of a government and having the effect of law

Regulation: A rule, having the effect of law, issued by a government department or agency

Speech: An oral presentation to a group of people, such as an address to a nation delivered by a president or other top official

Statute: A law passed by a legislative body

Tax Form: A legal document, filed with a local, state, or national government, usually four times or one time each year, showing tax-related information such as wages earned, taxes paid, taxes due, and other such information

Treaty: A document giving the details of an official agreement between two or more governments

Will: A legal document prepared by or for an individual describing that individual's wishes with regard to what is to happen with his or her money and property after his or her death

One famous historic document is a speech given by Pericles, the ruler of Athens, to honor soldiers who had died in the Peloponnesian War. One portion of the speech describes Greek democracy. Let's see how one student, Ada, answered a question about this part of the speech.

One Student's Response

We are called a democracy, for the [power] is in the hands of the many and not of the few. But while there exists equal justice to all…, the claim of excellence is also recognized; and when a citizen is in any way distinguished, he is preferred [for] public service, not as a matter of privilege, but as the reward of merit. Neither is poverty an obstacle, but a man may benefit his country [however poor or little known he may be]….[We are prevented from doing wrong by respect for the authorities and for the laws, having a particular regard [for] those laws which [exist to protect the powerless] as well as those unwritten laws which bring upon [those who break them the disrepute of their fellow citizens].

Excerpt from Pericles' Funeral Oration

1. According to Pericles, what advantages are there in a democratic form of government?

From reading the question, Ada knew that she needed to identify the advantages of democratic government described by Pericles. She read the document carefully and made an outline of the main idea and details. She reread the parts she had difficulty understanding the first time. After Ada had finished, she looked over her outline. Using her notes, Ada wrote, "One of the advantages of democracy, according to Pericles, is that it puts power in the hands of the many, not the few, and offers equal justice for all. It rewards citizens on the basis of merit but does not exclude the poor or unknown. It also encourages respect for the law, particularly those laws that exist to protect the powerless." Ada then reread her answer to make sure she had answered the question correctly.

What to Look for in Official Government Documents

Type and Purpose

Read the document carefully to learn what type of document it is (a treaty, a speech, etc.) and its purpose, or what it is about. As the chart on page 71 tells you, a speech is a an oral presentation to a group of people. The purpose of the speech by Pericles was to honor soldiers who had fought and died for Athenian democracy. The speech supports its purpose by including details about the benefits of democracy.

Main Idea

A **main idea** is what a document is mostly about. The main idea of the Pericles speech excerpt is that democracy is a beneficial form of government based on rule by the many.

Supporting Details

Supporting details are pieces of information that contribute to the main idea. The supporting details in a peace treaty, for example, might describe how two governments intend to keep the peace. In the example from Pretest A, supporting details about the positive features of democracy include equal justice for all, reward based on merit, and respect for the law.

How to Answer a Scaffolding Question about an Official Government Document

Read the question, paying close attention to key words that tell you what to do. Then study the document. Ask yourself what kind of document it is, what its purpose and main idea are, and what details support the main idea. Next, answer the question. Be sure to support your answer with examples from the document.

Strategy Review: Official Government Documents

- Figure out what the question is asking and what kind of document you are analyzing.
- Read the caption, if there is one.
- Determine the document's purpose and main idea.
- Look for details that support the main idea.
- Consider what you know about the time the document was written.
- Make sure you answer the whole question.

Exercise A: Thinking about Official Government Documents

Directions:

Use the strategies you just learned to analyze the following historical document. You will answer the following scaffolding question at the end of the exercise: What change did this document make in the official status of adults from Japan on U.S. territory?

Whereas it is provided by Section 21 of Title 50 of the United States Code as follows:

"Whenever there is a declared war between the United States and any foreign nation or government, or any invasion or predatory incursion is perpetrated, attempted, or threatened against the territory of the United States by any foreign nation or government, and the President makes public proclamation of the event, all natives, citizens, denizens, or subjects of the hostile nation or government, being of the age of fourteen years and upward, who shall be within the United States and not actually naturalized, shall be liable to be apprehended, restrained, secured, and removed as alien enemies...."

Now, therefore, I, Franklin D. Roosevelt, as President of the United States, and as Commander in Chief..., do hereby make public proclamation to all whom it may concern that an invasion has been perpetrated upon the territory of the United States by the Empire of Japan....

I do hereby further proclaim and direct that the conduct to be observed on the part of the United States toward all natives, citizens, denizens or subjects of the empire of Japan being of the age of fourteen years and upwards who shall be within the United States or within any territories in any way subject to the jurisdiction of the United States and not actually naturalized, who for the purpose of this Proclamation... are termed alien enemies, shall be as follows:...

---

from Presidential proclamation filed December 8, 1941

1. In your own words, what does the question ask?

_____

_____

Take notes about the document.

2. What is the document's purpose?

_____

_____

3. What is the main idea of the document?

_____

_____

4. What are some details that support the main idea?

_____

_____

5. **Answer the scaffolding question:** What does this document authorize, and for what reason?

_____

_____

Exercise B. Scaffolding Question Practice: Official Government Documents

Directions:

Answer the question that follows each excerpt from an historical document. Use the strategies from the lesson to analyze the documents.

> *Oh my warriors, whither would you flee? Behind you is the sea, before you, the enemy. You have left now only the hope of your courage and your constancy. Remember that in this country you are more unfortunate than the orphan seated at the table of the avaricious [greedy] master. Your enemy is before you, protected by an innumerable army; he has men in abundance, but you, as your only aid, have your own swords, and, as your only chance for life, such chance as you can snatch from the hands of your enemy. If…you delay to seize immediate success, your good fortune will vanish, and your enemies, whom your very presence has filled with fear, will take courage. Put far from you the disgrace from which you flee in dreams, and attack this monarch who has left his strongly fortified city to meet you. Here is a splendid opportunity to defeat him, if you will expose yourselves freely to death.*

Excerpt from a speech by Tarik to his soldiers during the conquest of Spain, 711 CE

1. What arguments does Tarik use to urge his soldiers to fight?

_____

_____

_____

> *They have killed and captured many, and have destroyed the churches and devastated the empire. If you permit them to continue…, the faithful of God will be much more widely attacked by them. On this account I, or rather the Lord, beseech you as Christ's heralds to publish this everywhere and to persuade all people of whatever rank, foot-soldiers and knights, poor and rich, to carry aid promptly to those Christians and to destroy that vile race from the lands of our friends. I say this to those who are present; it [is] meant also for those who are absent. Moreover, Christ commands it.*

Part of a speech by Pope Urban II, in 1095, calling for the Crusades

2. How does the Pope justify the call to war?

_____

_____

> *We have but one aim and one single irrevocable purpose. We are resolved to destroy Hitler and every vestige of the Nazi regime. From this nothing will turn us. Nothing. We will never parley; we will never negotiate with Hitler or any of his gang. We shall fight him by land; we shall fight him by sea; we shall fight him in the air, until, with God's help, we have rid the earth of his shadow and liberated its people from his yoke.*

Excerpt from radio address by Prime Minister Winston Churchill, after Germany invaded Russia, June 22, 1941

3. What kind of commitment does Great Britain have to defeating Nazi Germany, according to Churchill?

_____

_____

_____

MINI-DBQ: THE TERRORIST ATTACKS OF SEPTEMBER 11, 2001

Exercise A: Analyzing Sources

Directions:

Answer the question for each document.

A crowd gathers in India to read newspaper accounts of September 11 attacks on U.S.

1. How would you describe these people's reactions to the news of the September 11 attacks?

_____

_____

_____

_____

The British nation mourns for the people of the United States.

2. This photo is of British citizens. What is unusual about the photo? What does the photo tell you about British reaction to September 11?

_____

_____

_____

_____

_____

To the Congress of the United States

Pursuant to section 201 of the National Emergencies Act (50 U.S.C. 1621), I hereby report that I have exercised my authority to declare a national emergency by reason of the terrorist attacks at the World Trade Center, New York, New York, and the Pentagon, and the continuing and immediate threat of further attacks on the United States. A copy of my proclamation is attached.

Further, I have authorized, pursuant to section 12302 of title 10, United States Code, the Secretary of Defense, and the Secretary of Transportation, with respect to the Coast Guard when it is not operating as a service within the Department of the Navy, to order to active duty units and individual members not assigned to units of the Ready Reserve to perform such missions the Secretary of Defense may determine necessary. The deployment of United States forces to conduct operational missions in connection with the World Trade Center and Pentagon attacks necessitates this action.

A copy of my Executive Order implementing this action is attached.

GEORGE W. BUSH
THE WHITE HOUSE,
September 14, 2001

National Emergency declaration issued by President Bush three days after the terrorist attacks on the United States

3. What is the main idea of this document?

_____

_____

Exercise B: Writing about Related Sources

Directions:

Write a paragraph in response to the long-answer question below. Be sure to include at least three details from the documents in your answer. Reviewing your responses to the scaffolding questions will help you to answer the long-answer question as well.

Long-answer question: What were some of the consequences of the September 11, 2001 terrorist attacks?

_____

_____

_____

_____

_____

_____

_____

_____

_____

_____

_____

MINI-DBQ

LESSON 3.1: SENTENCE AND PARAGRAPH WRITING FOR THE SOCIAL STUDIES

As you have seen, DBQ tests usually contain two kinds of questions: scaffolding questions and essay questions. Scaffolding questions can usually be answered in one or two sentences. Occasionally, you might want to write three or four sentences to answer a scaffolding question completely. Essay questions require longer answers. The answers to essay questions usually require four to five paragraphs. In the next lesson, you will learn about the parts of a good essay. First, however, in this lesson you will learn how to write good sentences and the paragraphs that make up essays.

Writing Sentences

A **sentence** is a group of words that expresses a single complete idea. A sentence must contain at least one **subject** (what the sentence is about) and one **verb** (an action word that tells what the subject is doing or a state-of-being word such as *am, are, is, was, were,* or *be*).

EXAMPLES:

SUBJECT   VERB

The Black Death killed thousands in the 1330s and 1340s.

SUBJECT   VERB

Fleas spread bubonic plague from infected rats to people.

The following chart explains some important rules to keep in mind when writing sentences:

Guidelines for Writing Sentences

1. Make sure that every sentence contains a subject and a verb.
2. Make sure that every sentence begins with a capital letter.
3. Make sure that every sentence ends with an end mark—a period, a question mark, or an exclamation point.
4. Keep your sentences interesting by starting them in different ways and by writing sentences of different lengths.
   DULL: The plague came to Europe from China. In 1347, Italian traders returned from the Black Sea. The ships were full of goods from China. The sailors were dying of a disease. They brought the disease to Messina, Sicily. The Sicilians tried to drive them away from the city. The disease was already spreading through the countryside.

MORE INTERESTING: The plague came to Europe from China. It arrived in Europe aboard Italian merchant ships that had traveled from the Black Sea. When the ships landed in Sicily in 1347, many sailors were sick or dying from a mysterious disease. The Sicilians ordered the ships to leave Messina, but it was too late. The disease had already spread into the rural areas from the city.

5. Writings in social studies contain many **proper nouns**—names of people, places, and events. They also contain **proper adjectives**—descriptive words made from proper nouns. Make sure that you capitalize proper nouns and adjectives when writing your sentences.

INCORRECT: In the late 14th and 15th centuries, norse (scandinavian) settlers in greenland died off or abandoned their villages. Historians don't know whether climate changes, lack of trade, or disease (such as the plague) destroyed the settlements.

CORRECT: In the late 14th and 15th centuries, Norse (Scandinavian) settlers in Greenland died off or abandoned their villages. Historians don't know whether climate changes, lack of trade, or disease (such as the plague) destroyed the settlements.

6. Avoid sentence fragments—groups of words that do not contain a subject and a verb or that do not express a complete idea.

FRAGMENT: Painting the *Danse Macabre,* or the dance of death. (This group of words is missing a subject.)

COMPLETE SENTENCE: Artists began painting the *Danse Macabre,* or the dance of death.

7. Avoid run-on sentences—ones in which two sentences are run together without an end mark to separate them.

RUN-ON: Painters used symbols to remind people of death a picture of people going on a hunt, for example, might include a dead hunter riding a skeleton horse.

CORRECTED: Painters used symbols to remind people of death. A painting of people going on a hunt, for example, might include a dead hunter riding a skeleton horse.

8. Use quotation marks around words quoted directly from a source.

EXAMPLE: The Italian author Boccaccio, who survived an epidemic in 1348, said that plague victims often "ate lunch with their friends and dinner with their ancestors in paradise."

Writing Paragraphs

When you write an essay for a DBQ exam, the essay will be made up of several paragraphs (usually four or five). Therefore, it is a good idea for you to learn about proper paragraph form.

What Is a Paragraph?

A **paragraph** is a group of sentences about a single main idea. Read the example at the top of the next page.

Topic sentence — One of the most revered figures in Indian history is Mohandas K. Gandhi. Gandhi was born in 1869, when India was a colony of Great Britain. After becoming a lawyer, he practiced in South Africa. Indians living there were often referred to as "coolies." One day Gandhi was riding in the first-class compartment of a train when a white passenger ordered that the conductor "take this coolie out and put him in a lower class!" This experience of racial discrimination changed Gandhi's life. He developed nonviolent methods to protest racial prejudice based on the belief that "nonviolence is the greatest force at the disposal of mankind." Gandhi returned to India in 1914 and traveled the country encouraging peaceful resistance to British rule. Millions adopted his ideas of *ahimsa* (noninjury) and economic independence for India.

Body sentences

Clincher sentence — When he was assassinated in 1948, Indians mourned Gandhi as the father of their nation.

A well-written paragraph contains several parts, as follows:

Parts of a Paragraph

- The **topic sentence** gives the main idea of the paragraph.
- The **body sentences** provide details that support the main idea of the paragraph.
- The **clincher sentence** sums up the paragraph.

In the paragraph about Gandhi given above, the first sentence is the topic sentence. It tells you that the paragraph will be about Mohandas K. Gandhi and his importance to Indian history. The last sentence in the paragraph is the clincher sentence. It restates the main idea in different words. Each sentence between the topic sentence and the clincher sentence gives specific details about why Gandhi is honored for his role in Indian history.

You can think of a paragraph as being like a hamburger. The topic sentence is the bun on top. The clincher sentence is the bun on the bottom. The meat and all its dressings are the supporting details that appear in the middle of the paragraph.

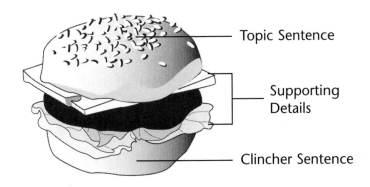

Topic Sentence

Supporting Details

Clincher Sentence

Follow these steps when writing a paragraph:

Writing a Paragraph, Step by Step

Step 1: Make a rough outline of the paragraph on scrap paper. Jot down the main idea that will be stated in your topic sentence. Then, beneath the main idea, use dashes to introduce your supporting details. In a paragraph on a DBQ test, your supporting details will be information from the documents you have studied.

Gandhi a revered figure in Indian history
—Born in 1869, when India was a British colony
—Became a lawyer and practiced in South Africa
—Indians discriminated against; called "coolies"
—Developed philosophy of nonviolence after being thrown off a train
—Believed that "nonviolence is the greatest force at the disposal of mankind"
—Returned to India in 1914 and led movement for independence
—Assassinated in 1948

This outline happens to contain a lot of supporting details. However, usually three or four supporting details will be enough.

Step 2: Look over your rough outline. Make sure that your supporting details are in a sensible order, such as chronological order or order of importance. If necessary, rearrange your details.

Step 3: Write the body sentences, following your outline. Try to vary the beginnings and the lengths of your sentences, and make sure that every sentence begins with a capital letter. If you wish to do so, quote directly from one or more of your source documents. Make sure to put direct quotations in quotation marks.

Step 4: Write a clincher sentence that restates the main idea of the paragraph in other words.

Step 5: Proofread the paragraph for errors. Reread it carefully. Make sure that you have
- indented the first line of the paragraph
- used complete sentences
- spelled each word correctly
- used a capital letter at the beginning of each sentence
- capitalized each proper noun or proper adjective
- used an end mark, such as a period, question mark, or exclamation point, at the end of each sentence.

There is an exception to the rules about writing paragraphs given above: When writing an essay, the first paragraph will be a special kind of paragraph known as an **introductory paragraph** or **introduction.** The form of the introductory paragraph will be a little different from that of the other paragraphs in your essay. You will learn more about introductory paragraphs in the next lesson.

Exercise A: Writing Good Sentences

Directions:

Rewrite the following sentences and passages, correcting the errors in them.

1. Confucius was born in northeastern China at the time of his birth in 551 BCE, rival princes were constantly fighting among themselves. (Correct the run-on sentence.)

_____

_____

_____

2. Confucius was poor, but he was. Determined to become a great scholar.

_____

_____

3. When confucius became a teacher, his best pupils lived with him.

_____

_____

4. Some of his pupils wrote down the master's sayings in a book called the analects.

_____

_____

5. Confucius believed that. Princes were thinking of themselves instead of what was best for their people.

_____

_____

_____

6. Confucius had an idea. His idea could bring peace to China. He thought princes needed well-educated advisers. These advisers could help princes act right Then the princes would not act selfishly. Confucius believed that anyone who loved learning would also be a good person. So he taught his students to love learning. He taught his students to act right. He encouraged his scholars to advise princes. He encouraged his pupils to help rulers carry out their policies. Confucius died in 479 BCE. His ideas influenced Chinese government for three centuries.

_____

_____

_____

_____

_____

_____

_____

_____

_____

Exercise B: Making an Outline

Directions:

Use information from the documents on page 7 to make a rough outline for a paragraph contrasting the way Confucius and Han Fei-tzu thought about government.

_____

_____

_____

_____

_____

Exercise C: Writing a Paragraph

Directions:

Write a paragraph based on the outline that you made for Exercise B. Make sure that your paragraph contains a topic sentence, several body sentences containing information from the documents on page 7, and a clincher sentence.

_____

_____

_____

_____

_____

_____

_____

_____

LESSON 3.1

LESSON 3.2: ESSAY WRITING FOR THE SOCIAL STUDIES

As you learned in Lesson 1.1, a DBQ test usually includes one or more essay questions. In this lesson, you will learn about the parts of a good essay.

What Is an Essay?

An **essay** is a group of paragraphs that work together to support a single main idea, or **thesis.** A good essay contains the following parts:

You can think of an essay as being like a building. The **topic** is what the essay is about. The **thesis statement** is the main idea of the essay. Together, the topic and the thesis statement are like the roof of the building. The body paragraphs in the essay are like the pillars or walls that hold up the roof. The conclusion is like the base of the building. Use the graphic organizer on the following page to plan an essay.

The Parts of an Essay

An essay contains three parts, as follows:

1. The **introduction** is a paragraph that catches the reader's attention. It also presents the main idea, or **thesis,** of the essay.
2. The **body,** which can be one or more paragraphs long, presents ideas that support the thesis. Many of the essays that you write for school will contain two or three body paragraphs or more.
3. The **conclusion** is a paragraph that sums up the ideas in the rest of the essay.

The Parts of an Essay

Introduction

Body

Conclusion

Graphic Organizer for Planning Essays

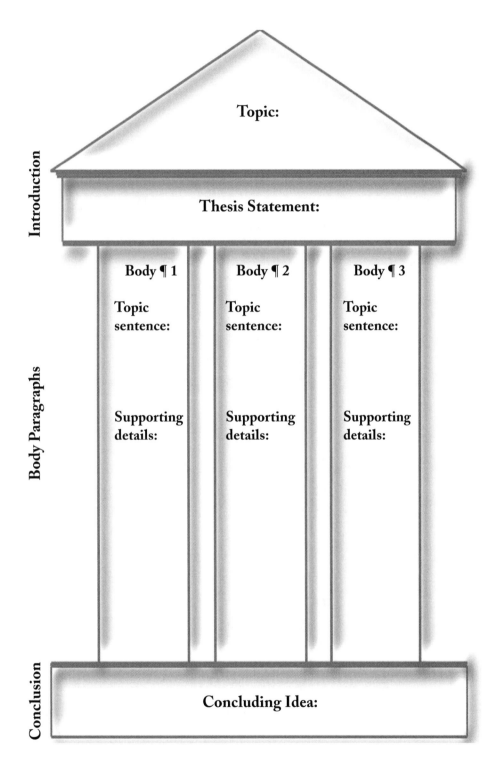

Introduction

Topic:

Thesis Statement:

Body Paragraphs

Body ¶ 1

Topic sentence:

Supporting details:

Body ¶ 2

Topic sentence:

Supporting details:

Body ¶ 3

Topic sentence:

Supporting details:

Conclusion

Concluding Idea:

On the following pages is an example of a completed essay about different ideas on good government. Before reading this sample essay, you might want to review the information and the document excerpts used in preparing this essay, which appear on pages 3–7.

One Student's Finished Essay

header —— Shawn Isenstein
February 22

○

title —— Ancient Roots of Democracy

paragraph 1,
introduction —— Abraham Lincoln needed only ten words to express the American ideal of government: "government of the people, by the people, for the people." These words from Lincoln's 1863 Gettysburg Address are so familiar that Americans can forget that people of other times had different ideas about democracy. In some countries, democracy was not even considered the best form of government. Ancient philosophers from Greece, Rome,

thesis
statement —— and China all believed that government should be "for the people," but they had very different ideas about what form of government was best.

○

Thinkers in ancient Greece developed several ideas that have become part of American democracy. In his Funeral Oration, Pericles explained how he expanded Athenian democracy in the fifth century BCE. Previously, a few wealthy citizens controlled the government. Pericles put political power "in the hands of the

first body
paragraph —— many and not of the few." He believed that all citizens should have equal rights under the law and equal opportunity to serve their state. In his criticism of the Spartan government, Aristotle noted that officials should not serve for life. He also argued that those who accept bribes are unfit for public office.

Cicero's ideas about government were shaped by Roman history. The first Romans were ruled by kings. In the sixth century BCE, Romans established a republic, a form of government in which citizens elect their leaders. When Cicero lived, the republic

○

second body
paragraph —— was ending, and the Roman Empire was beginning. Perhaps the times in which he lived gave Cicero a unique perspective. As he explained in <u>On the Republic,</u> he saw advantages to many forms

of government. A monarchy gives a king the power to protect his people. An oligarchy allows many talented aristocrats to govern. A democracy gives the most freedom to the people.

third body paragraph

Two Chinese philosophers debated whether the basis of government should be what is right or what works. Confucius argued that wise government is based on virtue, while Han Fei-tzu believed that effective government is based on law. Confucius admitted that fear of punishment would keep people from breaking the law. However, he believed that a leader should model good behavior and expect propriety from others. Han Fei-tzu rejected the idea that government should encourage people to become good. Since "not even ten persons can be counted on [to do good]," leaders should not try to encourage virtue. Instead, they should concentrate their efforts on a more effective way of maintaining order: enforcing good laws.

paragraph 5, conclusion

Each of these ancient cultures made contributions to our ideas about government. Athens was the birthplace of democracy. Rome created a republic. Chinese philosophers recognized the relationship between private behavior and public laws. This heritage shapes the way Americans think about what it means to have a government "of the people, by the people, for the people."

Understanding Essays: Purpose

An essay should accomplish a specific **purpose,** or goal. The chart below gives some examples of purposes that an essay can accomplish. Some essays have more than one of these purposes:

The Purpose of an Essay

An essay can accomplish any of these purposes:

To inform. An essay written to inform provides facts about the topic of the essay.

To persuade. An essay written to persuade presents an opinion and supports it.

To entertain. An essay written to entertain has as its major purpose creating an amusing or enjoyable experience for the reader.

To narrate. An essay written to narrate is one that tells a true story.

The essays that you write for DBQ tests will almost always be **informative essays,** ones that present facts about a topic.

Understanding Essays: Audience

An essay should be written with a particular **audience,** or group of readers, in mind. If you are writing an essay for children, you will use short sentences and simple words. If you are writing for an audience of adults, you will probably use longer sentences and more complicated words. When writing a DBQ essay, assume that you are writing for an audience of adults. However, do not assume that your audience already knows a lot about your topic. Write as though your audience were a group of intelligent adults who, nonetheless, do not know a lot about the topic you are writing about.

Understanding Essays: Organization

The body paragraphs in an essay should be well **organized.** That is, they should be presented in an order that makes sense. Some common ways to organize ideas in an essay are **time order, degree order,** and **spatial order:**

Organizing an Essay

Time order. Organize the ideas in the order in which they occurred. For example, if you were writing an essay about the life of Confucius, the first paragraph might be about his early life in Zou. That paragraph might be followed by one about his service as adviser to the prince of Lü. The next paragraph might be about his final years, which he spent teaching more than 3,000 students.

Degree order. Choose some characteristic of your subject, such as familiarity, value, or importance, and organize your piece from *less to more* or *more to less*. For example, you might organize the ideas by how important they seem to you, from most important to least important. Suppose that you are writing an essay about why the Aztec Empire fell. You might decide that the most important cause was the capture of its capital, Tenochtitlán, by Hernán Cortés in 1521. The next most important factor might be the willingness of the Aztecs' subjects to revolt against them; more than 150,000 fought with Cortés against their conquerors. Finally, you might write about the smallpox epidemic that killed half of the population of Tenochtitlán and left the city too weak to stand against the Spanish and their allies.

Spatial order. Organize the ideas according to location. For example, if you were writing about the spread of the Black Death, you might write about its beginnings in China, its arrival in Europe in 1347, and its spread to North Africa in 1348.

Of course, these are not the only reasonable ways to organize ideas in an essay. Any ordering of ideas that is reasonable—in which the ideas follow one another in a sensible, logical way—is acceptable.

Writing the Introduction of an Essay

The **introduction,** or opening paragraph, of an essay, should do two things. First, it should grab the attention of the reader. It should get him or her interested in the piece. Second, it should present the main idea, or **thesis statement,** of the essay. The thesis statement is probably the most important sentence in the essay because it sets forth what the rest of the essay will be about. Here are some ways to grab the attention of the reader:

Openers for Introductory Paragraphs

Begin with an interesting question:
—When Nelson Mandela was imprisoned on Robben Island, who would have expected him to become South Africa's first black president?
—Was the Vietnam War a foolish waste of lives or a necessary defense of freedom?

Begin with a quotation:
—In his *Meditations*, Marcus Aurelius writes, "Very little is needed to make a happy life. It is all within yourself, in your way of thinking."

> *Begin with a brief story:*
>   —According to an ancient story, the philosopher Chuang Chou once dreamed that he was a butterfly, flitting about from flower to flower. When he awoke, he thought, "Oh, I am no longer a butterfly but a man." Then, he thought, "Oh, perhaps I am a butterfly dreaming that he is a man." As this story shows, it is possible to doubt almost anything. Increasingly, scholars have come to doubt much of what was once believed about the history of Israel.
>
> *Begin with a startling or fascinating fact:*
>   —The Black Death killed one of every three people living in Europe during the 14th century.

After grabbing the attention of your reader, state your main idea, or thesis. This is the idea that you will support in the rest of your essay. In a DBQ essay, the thesis should be a general one-sentence or two-sentence answer to the DBQ essay question. Suppose, for example, that the DBQ question is based on a map of an ancient trade route running from China to Rome. The question might be:

> What was the importance of the Silk Road?

There are many possibilities for introductions based on this prompt. The following example begins with an interesting question and an analogy. Notice that it ends with a single sentence that states the thesis—a general answer to the essay question.

What was the ancient and medieval equivalent of the Internet? The Internet, of course, is the modern information super-highway—one of the principal means by which ideas, goods, and services are exchanged among distant cultures in our world today. From ancient times through the later Middle Ages, the equivalent of the Internet was the Silk Road, which allowed for exchanges of ideas and goods between China in the East and Central Asia in the West.

Writing the Body Paragraphs of an Essay

Each body paragraph, or paragraph found in the main part of an essay, should present one main idea that supports the thesis. This main idea is presented in the topic sentence of the paragraph. In a DBQ essay, the supporting details should come from the documents that you have been given.

Before writing a body paragraph, first make a quick rough outline of it. Jot down the main idea that will be used in the topic sentence. Then jot down the supporting details from the documents, introducing each with a dash.

The following are examples of a rough outline and a finished body paragraph.

Notes in Rough Outline Form

Silk Road connected peoples of the ancient world
—Taklimakan and Gobi Deserts natural barriers
—Himalaya and Pamir Mountains also prevented contact
—had three major routes
—northern route ran to Black Sea
—central route ran through Persia and Mediterranean to Rome
—southern route went through Afghanistan to India

Sample Body Paragraph

Before the Silk Road was opened, people from China and the Mediterranean region were separated by natural barriers. One barrier was the harsh Taklimakan Desert, which people who live in Central Asia call "the Land of Death." Another barrier was the largest mountains in the world, which include the Himalayas and the Pamir range. As people discovered ways across these barriers, the Silk Road developed three major east-west routes. The northern route linked China to the Black Sea. The central route ran 4,000 miles through Persia and the Mediterranean to Rome. The southern route crossed Afghanistan and ended in India.

Writing the Conclusion of an Essay

The conclusion, or end, of the essay should be a single paragraph. In this paragraph, you should restate the main ideas from your body paragraphs in other words. Then, end by restating, in other words, the main idea, or thesis, of the essay. See the sample concluding paragraph in the essay on pages 88–89.

Exercise A: Analyzing an Essay

Directions:

Reread the sample essay by Shawn Isenstein on pages 88–89. Then answer the following questions about it.

1. What is the thesis statement of the essay? Where does the thesis statement appear?

_____

_____

_____

2. What method did Shawn use to grab the reader's attention in the opening of the essay?

_____

_____

3. What is the topic sentence of the first body paragraph (the second paragraph in the essay)?

_____

_____

4. What is the topic sentence of the second body paragraph (the third paragraph in the essay)?

_____

_____

5. What is the topic sentence of the third body paragraph (the fourth paragraph in the essay)?

_____

_____

6. How did the writer organize the ideas in this essay?

_____

_____

7. In what places in the essay did Shawn quote from sources? What sources did Shawn quote from?

_____

_____

_____

8. Did Shawn use all the source documents from pages 3–7 in the essay? Explain.

_____

_____

_____

Exercise B: Outlining a Body Paragraph

Directions:

Choose one body paragraph from the essay on pages 88–89. Write a rough outline of it.

_____

_____

_____

_____

_____

Exercise C: Planning an Essay

Directions:

Choose a topic from current events reported in the newspaper. Find two or three newspaper articles or graphics about the topic. If you wish, you can use one Internet source as well. Study your sources, then make a complete plan for an essay about the topic. Fill in the following form to show what you plan to do in the introduction and body of your essay.

Topic of Essay: _____

Purpose:_____

Audience:_____

Method of Organization:_____

Introduction

Thesis Statement:_____

Method for Grabbing Reader's Attention:_____

Body Paragraph 1

Topic Sentence:_____

Supporting Details:_____

Body Paragraph 2

Topic Sentence:_____

Supporting Details:_____

Body Paragraph 3

Topic Sentence:_____

Supporting Details:_____

The conclusion will restate, in different words, the topic sentences from the body of the essay and the thesis statement from the introduction.

Exercise D: Writing an Essay

Directions:

On your own paper, write a draft of the essay that you planned in Exercise C. Make sure that your essay has an introduction, a body, and a conclusion.

Exercise E: Proofreading an Essay

Directions:

Reread your draft essay, proofreading it for errors. Follow the checklist for proofreading given below.

Proofreading Symbols

Symbol and Example	Meaning of Symbol
∧ bicycle built for two	Insert (add) something that is missing.
⌐ Paris in the ~~the~~ spring	Delete (cut) these letters or words.
— extreme ~~estreme~~ skiing	Replace this letter or word.
∿ the glass delicate slippers	Transpose (switch) the order.
⌐o give to the needy gifts	Move this word to where the arrow points.
⌒ chair person	Close up this space.
⌶ truely	Delete this letter and close up the space.
≡ five portuguese sailors	Capitalize this letter.
/ a lantern and a Sleeping bag	Lowercase this letter.
¶ waves. "Help me!" she cried.	Begin a new paragraph
⊙ All's well that ends well ⊙	Put a period here.
∧ parrots macaws, and toucans	Put a comma here.
∨ childrens toys	Put an apostrophe here.
ⓞ There are three good reasons	Put a colon here.
# the grandopening	Put a space here.

LESSON 3.3: WRITING YOUR OWN DBQ ESSAY, STEP BY STEP

Now it is your turn to write a DBQ essay. This lesson will take you step-by-step through the process, from notes to completed essay. You will write an essay in response to the question in Pretest A.

Although you already answered scaffolding questions and wrote an essay in Pretest A, by using the strategies you have learned and following this process, you will see how much you have improved!

Exercise A: Notetaking

Directions:

Reread the DBQ essay question for Pretest A, on page 2 of this book. Then, review the documents from Pretest A on pages 3–7. As you review the documents, take notes on the lines provided below.

Notes on selection from Pericles' Funeral Oration

_____

_____

_____

_____

Notes on Plato's Allegory of the Beast in _The Republic_

_____

_____

_____

Notes on excerpt from _The Politics of Aristotle_

_____

_____

_____

Notes on selection from Cicero's *On the Republic*

_____

_____

_____

Notes on selection from Emperor Claudius's Speech

_____

_____

_____

Notes on Map of the Roman Empire

_____

_____

_____

Notes on Chinese Sages

_____

_____

_____

Exercise B: Analyzing the Essay Question

Directions:

Reread the essay question from Pretest A, which appears on page 2. Then answer the following questions about it.

1. In your own words, what does the question ask you to write about?

_____

_____

2. What three parts must you include in your essay?

_____

_____

_____

Exercise C: Writing a Thesis Statement

Now that you know what the question asks, it is time to write a thesis statement. Remember that the thesis statement should be a general, one-sentence answer to the essay question.

_____

_____

Exercise D: Making a Rough Outline

Now, make a rough outline for the body of your essay on the following lines.

First Body Paragraph
Topic:

_____

Supporting Detail 1:

_____

Supporting Detail 2:

_____

Other Supporting Details:

_____

Second Body Paragraph

Topic:

_____

Supporting Detail 1:

_____

Supporting Detail 2:

_____

Other Supporting Details:

_____

_____

Third Body Paragraph

Topic:

_____

Supporting Detail 1:

_____

Supporting Detail 2:

_____

Other Supporting Details:

_____

_____

Conclusion

The conclusion will restate, in different words, the topic sentences from the body of the essay and the thesis statement from the introduction.

Exercise E: Writing and Proofreading the Essay

Now that you have a completed outline, it is time to write the essay. Use the lines on the next two pages and additional paper as necessary. After you are finished, read over the essay and correct any errors that you find in spelling, grammar, usage, capitalization, or punctuation. Refer to the proofreading checklist on page 97. Also check any quotations that you have used to make sure that they are word-for-word.

POSTTESTS

This unit contains two Posttests.

You will have an hour and a half to complete each test.

POSTTEST A: DOCUMENT-BASED QUESTION

Historical Background:

The Middle Ages in Europe began with the fall of the Roman Empire, around 500 CE, and lasted until the early 1400s CE. During the medieval age, most of Europe was fragmented into feudal kingdoms. Classical learning declined, and the power of the Roman Catholic Church grew. These changes had a great impact on European society, including the status of women. In general, women were considered inferior to men, but views were sometimes contradictory. The Church, for example, taught that women were beneath men but also said that they were more spiritually pure. According to the code of chivalry, knights were required to respect and even worship women. Although women were denied many rights, they were also placed on a pedestal. Study these documents to learn more about the role of women in medieval Europe.

Task:

Write an essay about women in medieval Europe. In your essay, discuss the roles of women and evaluate their position in medieval European society.

Before writing your essay, study the documents that follow and answer the scaffolding questions about them.

Part A: Scaffolding Questions

Directions:

Using information from the documents and your knowledge of social studies, answer the question that follows each document. Your answers will help you write the essay in Part B.

In April, with the cows in milk again, the peasant's wife was kept busy making butter and cheese and saving up the payment of eggs due to the lord at Easter.

1. How do the tasks performed by women and men differ in this painting?

_____

_____

> *You should mix the works of the active life with spiritual works...For you shall sometimes be busy with [the worldly life], to regulate and govern the household, your children, your servants, your neighbours, and your tenants...And you should also check and wisely ensure that your possessions and worldly goods are rightly cared for by your servants...At other times you shall...leave the bustle of the world and sit down at the feet of Our Lord in humility in prayers...And so you shall profitably go from one to the other, deserving reward and fulfil both, and then you keep the order of charity well.*

Excerpt from *Epistle of the Mixed Life,* a fourteenth-century book

2. What two basic roles does the author believe women should fulfill?

_____

_____

When you go to town or to church, you should be accompanied by companions suitable to your social position and especially by respectable women. Avoid questionable associates, and never go near a suspicious woman or allow one in your company. Keep your head straight, your eyelids decently lowered and motionless, and your gaze eight feet directly in front of you and on the ground without looking around at any man or woman to the right or left, or looking up, or shifting your gaze unsteadily from place to place, or laughing, or stopping to talk to anyone in the street.

Excerpt from *Le Ménagier de Paris,* a fourteenth-century book on housekeeping

4. What does this illustration imply about the role of medieval women?

_____

_____

_____

_____

In a comfortable home, an ailing burgher takes a nap while his meal is prepared by his wife and her servant.

3. How was a respectable medieval woman expected to behave in public?

_____

_____

_____

_____

_____

Knights courting ladies in a romantic garden.

5. What does the painting reveal about relations between upper-class men and women?

_____

_____

> *By marriage, the husband and wife are one person in law; that is, the very being or legal existence of the woman is suspended during the marriage, or at least is incorporated and consolidated into that of the husband; under whose wing, protection, and cover she performs every thing....A man cannot grant anything to his wife, or enter into covenant with her: for the grant would be to suppose her separate existence.*

Excerpt from eighteenth-century text about medieval marriage law

6. What is the author's main point about the status of women in marriage?

_____

_____

> *It seems to me that it is the duty of every princess and high-born lady... to excel in goodness, wisdom, manners, temperament and conduct, so that she can serve as an example on which other ladies and all other women can model their behaviour. Thus it is fitting that she should be devoted to God and have a calm, gentle and tranquil manner, restrained in her amusements and never intemperate [excessive].*

Excerpt from *Le Livre des Trois Virtus* (*The Book of Three Virtues*), by Christine de Pizan

7. What responsibility did a noble woman have, according to the author?

_____

_____

Nuns in a choir

A page from a fifteenth-century book of psalms

8. Why might medieval women choose to become nuns?

_____

_____

Part B: Essay Response

Directions:

Use your answers from Part A to write an essay about women in medieval Europe. In your essay, discuss the roles of women and evaluate their position in European society.

In your essay, remember to include
- an introductory paragraph stating your response to the question;
- three body paragraphs that support your response with information from the documents;
- a concluding paragraph.

_____

_____

_____

_____

_____

_____

_____

_____

_____

_____

_____

_____

_____

_____

_____

_____

_____

_____

_____

_____

_____

_____

_____

_____

_____

_____

_____

_____

_____

_____

_____

_____

_____

POSTTEST B: DOCUMENT-BASED QUESTION

Historical Background:

Islam is one of the world's great religions. With more than a billion followers, it is the second largest faith in the world and is growing rapidly. Islamic civilization is renowned for great achievements in art, literature, and the sciences. At the height of Islamic rule, Muslim leaders established peaceful, prosperous, and tolerant empires across vast territories. Yet today the world of Islam stands at a crossroads. While moderate Muslims hope to promote modern democratic rule in the Islamic world, Muslim radicals—often called fundamentalists—seek to create religious regimes with little concern for democratic rights. Study these documents to learn more about the religion and culture of Islam, and its compatibility with democracy.

Task:

Write an essay about Islam and democracy. In your essay, discuss the features of Islam and consider whether Islam is compatible with the principles of democracy.

Before you write your essay, study the documents that follow and answer the scaffolding questions about them.

Part A: Scaffolding Questions

Using information from the documents and your knowledge of social studies, answer the question that follows each document. Your answers will help you write the essay in Part B.

Studying the Quran in Uzbekistan. Islam is enjoying a revival in Central Asia after decades of Soviet rule.

1. What does this photo indicate about the study of Islam?

_____

_____

> One day, while we were sitting with [Muhammad], there came upon us a man whose clothes were exceedingly white and whose hair was exceedingly black....."Oh, Muhammad, tell me about Islam," he said. [Muhammad] replied: "Islam means to bear witness that there is no god but Allah, that Muhammad is the Messenger of Allah, to maintain the [required] prayers, to pay the poor-tax, to fast [in the month of] Ramadan, and to perform the pilgrimage to [Mecca] if you are able to do so."

Excerpt from the Hadith of Gabriel, a sixth-century statement of Muslim faith

2. What are the basic requirements of Islam?

_____

_____

Women wearing the *burqa,* a type of veil used in Afghanistan.

3. What relationship, if any, does the veil have to women's rights in Muslim societies?

_____

_____

> [E]galitarianism [equality] in Islam is more pronounced than in any other religion in the world. There are no caste systems, no priests, no differences between rich and poor in Islam....In numerous ways the Prophet emphasized that all human beings—men and women, rich and poor, black and white, Arab and non-Arab—are equal before God.

Excerpt from *Living Islam,* by Akbar S. Ahmed

4. How might Islam's emphasis on equality influence the development of democracy?

_____

_____

1920s poster showing Mustafa Kemal Ataturk, the first president of the Republic of Turkey. He introduced a series of political, social, legal, economic, and cultural reforms that transformed his country. Before that, however, he played a key role in the first genocide of modern times—the mass killings of Christian Armenians.

5. What Western influences does this poster show?

_____

_____

> Of all the challenges facing democracy in the 1990s, one of the greatest lies in the Islamic world. Only a handful of the more than four dozen predominantly Muslim countries have made significant strides toward establishing democratic systems. Among this handful...not one has yet achieved full, stable, or secure democracy. And the largest single regional bloc holding out against the global trend toward political pluralism comprises the Muslim countries of the Middle East and North Africa.

Excerpt from "Islam and Liberal Democracy," by Robin Wright, in *Journal of Democracy*, 1996

6. What problem does the author point out?

_____

_____

Of the 14 Middle Eastern countries, only Israel and Turkey are electoral democracies. Does this mean that Islam is inherently incompatible with democracy? Not so, says [Freedom House president Adrian] Karatnycky, as he points to democratic ferment in such countries across the Islamic world as Albania, Bangladesh, Djibouti, the Gambia, Indonesia, Mali, Niger, Nigeria, Senegal, Sierra Leone, and Turkey.

And in India, 150 million Muslims, the world's second-largest Muslim community, live under a democratically elected government. Karatnycky continues, "Important, though halting and inconsistent, inroads toward democratic reform have been made in several Arabic countries."

As novelist Salman Rushdie suggested recently in The New York Times, *the questioning by moderate Muslims of extremist "Islamism" is on the rise. "If Islam is to be reconciled with modernity, these voices must be encouraged until they swell into a roar."*

Excerpt from "Freedom Marches Undaunted," by John Hughes, *Christian Science Monitor,* 2001

7. Why is the author encouraged about the prospects for democracy in the Muslim world?

_____

_____

The Kuwait Parliament was established in 1961. Kuwait's experiment with democracy has influenced other countries in the region.

8. What does the photograph reveal about Kuwait?

_____

_____

Spectrum of Governments in the Islamic World

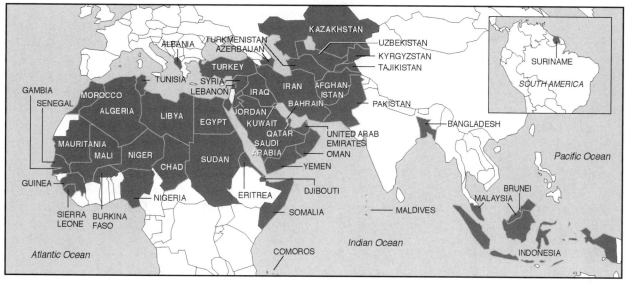

Countries with majority Muslim populations have greatly varying forms of government (as of 2002), ranging from democracy to monarchy and theocracy.

DEMOCRACY

Characterized by direct, free elections without restrictions on political parties; includes both parliamentary and republican systems. **Bangladesh, Senegal, Sierra Leone, Suriname, Turkey.**

EMERGING DEMOCRACY

Constitution provides for democratic, multiparty rule, but notable deficiencies remain. **Albania, Gambia, Indonesia, Lebanon, Niger.**

LIMITED DEMOCRACY

Includes direct elections of at least one branch of legislature, but characterized by authoritarian rule with leaders elected by referendum or overwhelming majorities. Some had recent elections marred by opposition boycotts or serious irregularities. **Algeria, Azerbaijan, Burkina Faso, Chad, Djibouti, Egypt, Guinea, Kazakhstan, Kyrgyzstan, Maldives, Mali, Mauritania, Tajikistan, Tunisia, Turkmenistan, Uzbekistan, Yemen.**

AUTHORITARIAN

Military or other authoritarian rule, with no elections or merely nominal ones. **Iraq, Libya, Syria.**

MONARCHY

Based on hereditary rule, with no elected legislative body; an asterisk denotes movement toward greater openness, with parliamentary elections planned within two years, or limited democratic experimentation under way. **Bahrain, Brunei, Oman, Qatar, Saudi Arabia, United Arab Emirates.**

MONARCHY/LIMITED DEMOCRACY

Based on hereditary rule, but with an elected parliament with some power. **Jordan, Kuwait, Malaysia, Morocco.**

THEOCRACY

Supreme leadership based on religious criteria, even if elections and some democracy coexist. **Iran.**

TRANSITIONAL

From military rule to civilian rule, as in Nigeria; or democratic practices suspended by seizure of power, as in Pakistan; or a transition government in place, but without full control of territory, as in **Afghanistan, Comoros, Eritrea, Nigeria, Pakistan, Somalia, Sudan.**

9. What is the most common type of government in the Islamic world? Describe that form of government in your own words.

_____

_____

_____

> *Iran is at a pivotal moment. Twenty-two years after a revolution that installed a conservative Islamic form of government, its very underpinnings are challenged by the forces of globalization, demographic change—two-thirds of Iranians are under 30—and secularism. Iranians of all stripes are struggling to define democracy within an Islamic system.*
>
> *[President] Khatami, a moderate cleric, says Iran must liberalize that system or risk alienating people altogether. While some opponents say he is too radical and some say he is too cautious, the majority of citizens support him.*
>
> *Khatami was swept to power four years ago with 69 percent of the vote. But despite his huge popularity, he has operated more like an opposition leader than a chief executive. Ultimate power under the Constitution lies in the hands of the supreme clerical leader, Ayatollah Ali Khamenei, who in the last year has increasingly supported the president's opponents. While Khatami has eased the social atmosphere and preached greater freedom of expression and religious democracy, his opponents kept a grip on key power centers, including the judiciary, security forces, state broadcasting, and a conservative body that can veto legislation by the reformist-dominated parliament.*

Excerpt from "Uneasy Mix: Islam, Democracy," Michael Theodoulou, *Christian Science Monitor*, June 5, 2001

10. What political conflicts does the author highlight in Iran?

_____

_____

_____

Part B: Essay Response

Directions:

Use your answers from Part A to write an essay about Islam and democracy. In your essay, discuss the features of Islam and consider whether Islam is compatible with democratic principles.

In your essay, remember to include
- an introductory paragraph stating your response to the question;
- three body paragraphs that support your response with information from the documents;
- a concluding paragraph.

STOP

Text Acknowledgments

p. 3, excerpt from Pericles' Funeral Oration, translated by Richard Hooker. p. 4 (top), ©1998 by the Internet Applications Laboratory at the University of Evansville. p. 4 (bottom), from Aristotle, The Politics of Aristotle, trans. Benjamin Jowett (London: Colonial Press, 1900). p. 5, from Oliver J. Thatcher, ed., The Library of Original Sources (Milwaukee: University Research Extension Co., 1907), Vol. III: The Roman World. p. 6 (top), from Tacitus: Annals, Book 11, translated by Alfred John Church and William Jackson Brodribb. p. 7 (top and bottom), excerpt translated by Michael Neville, from Reading About the World, Volume 1, edited by Paul Brians, et al., published by Harcourt Brace Custom Publishing. p. 12, ©1999 The Holocaust History Project (www.holocaust-history.org). p. 13 (top), from "Trials of War Criminals Before the Nuremberg Military Tribunals", Washington, U.S Government Printing Office, 1949–1953, Vol. XIII, p. 269–272. p. 13 (bottom), ©1999 The Holocaust History Project (www.holocaust-history.org). p. 15 (bottom), from The Diary of Anne Frank: The Critical Edition by Anne Frank, ©1986 by Anne Frank-Fonds, Basle/ Switzerland, for all texts of Anne Frank. Used by permission of Doubleday, a division of Random House, Inc. p. 55, Library of Congress, "California as I Saw It: First-Person Narratives of California's Early Years, 1849–1900." p. 57, from "What Did You Do in the War, Grandma?" to South Kingston High School, The Rhode Island Historical Society, and The Brown University Scholarly Technology Group. p. 59 (bottom), Ginger's Diary (www.gingersdiary.com) excerpt courtesy of B.Z. Leonard. p. 60 (top), from The Diary of Anne Frank: The Critical Edition by Anne Frank, ©1986 by The Anne Frank-Fonds, Basel/ Switzerland, for all texts of Anne Frank. Used by permission of Doubleday, a division of Random House, Inc. p. 60 (bottom), Letter from unidentified young woman, dated July 7, 1942, to Elizabeth Bayley Willis, Elizabeth Bayley Willis Papers, University of Washington Libraries (www.lib.washington.edu). pp. 61–62, selections from Letter to President Franklin D. Roosevelt, by Albert Einstein; Trinity Test Eyewitness Account, by Enrico Fermi; and Year of Decisions, by President Harry S Truman. The Nuclear Age Peace Foundation, PMB 121, 1187 Coast Village Road, California, 93108-2794 (www.nuclearfiles. org). p. 66, ©Tribune Media Services, Inc. All Rights Reserved. Reprinted with permission. p. 67, ©2001 by the New York Times Co., Reprinted by permission. p. 68, "Coalition-Building: U.S. Asks Rest of World to Join Terrorism Fight" by Edward Epstein in San Francisco Chronicle, Reprinted with permission. ©2001 The San Francisco Chronicle. p. 69 (top), "After Afghanistan: Is Iraq next?" by Peter Ford in Christian Science Monitor, and is reproduced with permission. ©2001 The Christian Science Monitor (www.csmonitor.com). All rights reserved. p. 69 (bottom), ©2001 by the New York Times Co., Reprinted by permission. p. 71, excerpt from Pericles' Funeral Oration. Translated by Richard Hooker. p. 73, Declarations of a State of War with Japan, Germany, and Italy, Part 7 by the President of the United States of America, A Proclamation. p. 74, from: Charles F. Horne, ed., The Sacred Books and Early Literature of the East (New York: Parke, Austin, & Lipscomb, 1917), Vol. VI: Medieval Arabia, pp. 241–242. p. 75 (top), from August. C. Krey, The First Crusade: The Accounts of Eyewitnesses and Participants, (Princeton: 1921), 42–43. p. 75 (bottom), Minister Winston Churchill's Broadcast on the Soviet-German War London, June 22, 1941, British Library of Information. p. 77 (bottom), The White House. p. 106 (bottom), ©1999 from Medical Gentlewoman, Life in a Gentry Household in the Later Middle Ages by Fiona Swabey. Reproduced by permission of Routledge, Inc., part of The Taylor & Francis Group. p. 107 (top), from "A Medieval Home Companion: Housekeeping in the Fourteenth Century" Translated and edited by Tania Bayard. ©1991 Harper Collins Publishers. p. 108 (bottom), from "Women in the Middle Ages" by Frances and Joseph Gies. ©1978 Thomas Y. Crowell Company. p. 109 (top), Christine de Pizan, Le Livre des Trois Vertus (The Book of Three Virtues). Translation by Kathy Garay and Madeleine Jeay, taken from the Medieval Women Website: http://mw.mcmaster.ca/scriptorium/cdpizan2.html. p. 113, from "The Oxford History of Islam" edited by John L. Esposito. ©1999 Oxford University Press. p. 114, from Living Islam by Akbar S. Ahmed. Original English Language Version ©1993 by Akbar S. Ahmed. Reprinted by permission of Facts On File, Inc. p. 115, Wright, Robin. Islam and Liberal Democracy: Two Visions of Reformation. Journal of Democracy 7:2 (1996), 64–75. ©The Johns Hopkins University Press and National Endowment for Democracy. Reprinted by permission of the Johns Hopkins University Press. p. 116 (top), "Freedom Marches Undaunted" by John Hughes in Christian Science Monitor, 2001 and is reproduced with permission. ©2001 The Christian Science Monitor (www.csmonitor.com). All rights reserved. p. 118, ©2001 Michael Theodoulou.

Art Acknowledgments

p. 11, Margaret Bourke-White/Timepix. p. 12 (top), Mansell/ Timepix. p. 14, from "Auschwitz: Technique and Operation of the Gas Chambers," J.C. Pressac, the Beate Klarsfeld Foundation, NY, 1989, p. 420. Photo Courtesy of Daniel Keren. p. 15 (top), Brown Brothers. p. 20, Margaret Bourke-White/Timepix. p. 23, ©Hulton Archive/Getty Images. p. 25 (bottom), ©Royal Geographical Society, London. p. 26 (top), ©Bettmann/ CORBIS. p. 26–27, ©Hulton Archive/Getty Images. p. 28, Letterpress with wood engraving, 1858 Unknown printer for Whiteley, Fassler & Kelly (Springfield, OH) 18" x 8". Wisconsin Historical Society. p. 32, ©Christie's Images/CORBIS. p. 33, Color lithograph, ca. 1925 Printed by Rozanicowski I Drug D.D. (Zagreb, Yugoslavia) for International Harvester Co. (Chicago) 31.5" x 22", Wisconsin Historical Society. p. 34, ©CORBIS. p. 35–37, ©Bettmann/CORBIS. p. 39, www.Boondocksnet.com. p. 41, www.Boondocksnet.com. p. 43, www.Boondocksnet.com. p. 44, from London Daily Chronicle, New York World Sunday Magazine, Nov. 26, 1905. p. 45, The Granger Collection, New York. p. 46–47, www.Boon-docksnet.com. p. 76, ©Reuters NewMedia Inc./CORBIS. p. 77 (top), ©AFP/CORBIS. p. 106 (top), ©The Pierpont MorganLibrary/Art Resource, NY. p. 107 (bottom), ©Foto Marburg/Art Resource, NY. p. 108 (top), North Wind Picture Archives. p. 109 (bottom), Nuns in choir, Franciscan Poor Clares, from a fifteenth-century psalter, MS Cott. Dom. A XVII, f. 74v, by permission of the British Library. p. 113 (top), ©REZA/Gamma Press. p. 114 (top), ©Reuters NewMedia Inc./CORBIS. p. 115 (top), The Granger Collection, New York. p. 116 (bottom), ©Reuters NewMedia Inc./CORBIS. p. 117, NYT Graphics.

Maps created by Sanderson Design, 2002.

INDEX

INDEX

INDEX OF TOPICS/THEMES

INDEX OF TOPICS/THEMES